THE
$AVE
MONEY
&EAT
WELL
COOKBOOK

THE $AVE MONEY

& EAT WELL COOKBOOK

Neil Gallagher

Bethany Fellowship INC.
MINNEAPOLIS, MINNESOTA 55438

Copyright © 1978
Neil Gallagher
All rights reserved

Published by Bethany Fellowship, Inc.
6820 Auto Club Road, Minneapolis, Minnesota 55438

Printed in the United States of America

Library of Congress Cataloging in Publication Data

Gallagher, Neil, 1941-
    The save money & eat well cookbook.

    Includes index.
    1. Cookery.   I. Title.
TX652.G34   641.5   78-12445
ISBN 0-87123-499-8

FOREWORD

In the beginning of her celebrated book, *Good Cheap Food*, Miriam Ungerer says:

> To the frequently asked question: "Did you make up all these recipes yourself?" The answer is "No." And neither does any other cookbook writer. Cooking is an evolutionary art proceeding simultaneously in many kitchens, and even when you do hit on something you think is original, chances are you'll find something very like it in the *Larousse Gastronomique*. I've invented some of the things in this book; others are my interpretation of classic dishes. In some instances I have adapted recipes for thrift, but never so much so that the character of the dish is ruined.
>
> *Good Cheap Food*, Viking Press, New York, 1973

I agree. However, I adapted no recipes from *Good Cheap Food*. There is a reason for that.

Some cookbooks (and *Good Cheap Food* is probably less guilty than others) project pretty weird ideas about "cheap" food. For them a "cheap" recipe is one using domestic sherry instead of imported sherry, sirloin cuts instead of filet, and fresh avocados instead of frozen. Those *are* cheap recipes if you live in the $25,000-$50,000 + income bracket.

The recipes in this book arose from living in the $5,000-$10,000 income bracket. They are for Joe Lunchpail and Joanne Budget. They're meant to keep you alive and comfortably ahead of bill collectors.

I am indebted to Dr. Margaret L. Ross (nutritionist) for her assistance in the selection and collection of these recipes.

ABOUT THE AUTHOR

Neil Gallagher was born in New York and educated in Massachusetts and Rhode Island. He served in Northern Thailand as a Peace Corps teacher and medic in leper colonies during which service he received the Thai Foreign Service Award. In 1966 he was elected to Outstanding Young Men of America.

He has written twenty-five professional and popular articles, including articles for *Philosophy and Phenomenonological Research*, *The Journal of Psychology and Theology,* and *The Christian Science Monitor,* and three books, *How to Stop the Porno Plague, Don't Go Overseas Until You've Read This Book,* and *How to Save Money on Almost Everything.*

He holds a Bachelor's Degree in History, an M.A. in Religion, and an M.A. in Philosophy. Following Ph.D. studies in a joint program of Philosophy and Psychiatry at the University of Cincinnati Graduate School and College of Medicine, he taught at the Victoria College, leaving to devote more time to a pulpit ministry and ministry of writing.

CONTENTS

KITCHEN BASICS

 3 teaspoons equal 1 tablespoon
 4 tablespoons equal 1/4 cup
16 tablespoons equal 1 cup
 5 tablespoons plus 1 teaspoon equal 1/3 cup
 2 cups equal 1 pint
 4 cups equal 1 quart
 4 quarts equal 1 gallon
 2 cups butter, solid, equal 1 pound
 1/2 cup butter, solid, equals 1/4 pound
 2 cups granulated sugar equal 1 pound
 2 1/2 cups powdered sugar equal 1 pound
 3 1/2 cups confectioner's sugar equal 1 pound
 4 cups flour equal 1 pound
 1/4 cup cocoa (4 tablespoons) equal 1 ounce
 2 tablespoons butter equal 1 ounce
 1 square chocolate equals 1 ounce

OVEN TEMPERATURES

Slow—250° to 300°
Moderate—325° to 375°
Hot—400° to 450°
Very Hot—475° and above

SAVING MONEY ON BUYING AND PREPARING THE BASIC FOUR

Breads and Cereals

Find a bakery with a day-old discount or thrift-store section. Buy twenty loaves of bread at a time, providing your freezer has room. You save money and frequent trips to the store which saves gas money and wear and tear on the car. A 1½-lb. loaf of fresh bread runs 50¢-60¢ per loaf. The same 1½-lb. loaf of day-old runs 20¢-25¢ per loaf. For the price of two loaves of fresh bread, you can buy up to five loaves of day-old. Incidentally, if you buy fresh bread, it's usually a couple of days before the whole loaf is eaten—and then it's day-old.

Some cereals are all right if you buy selectively. Prices vary enormously. A family of five eating from "variety-pack" individual cartons gets ten servings (each)—a total of fifty servings—for $9.49. The family eating cooked cereal, gets ten servings each—a total of fifty servings—for $1.25. Lay off sugared cereals entirely. Besides ruining teeth and putting on empty calories, it costs about 6¢ per serving. Unsweetened dry cereals cost about 3¢ per serving; cooked cereals about 1½¢ per serving.

Dairy Products

Milk: Buy powdered milk in large boxes. It will keep for a long time if container is kept closed and dry. A quart of fresh milk costs about 40¢, powdered, 20¢. If you tire of its taste, add chocolate. Don't use the expensive "Instant Chocolate Drink" mixes. Instead, mix cocoa half and half with sugar, dissolve with a touch of hot water (tap water will do) and add three, four or five tablespoons of powdered milk to make one glass (to taste). If family members just don't like the taste of powdered milk, try this: Use powdered milk for cooking, and mix drinking milk half and half with whole milk. It tastes better and saves money.

Eggs: Scan yellow pages and classified ads for poultry farms that sell direct.

Margarine and butter: Buy in pound blocks and cut into quarters yourself. When on sale, buy several and freeze.

Meat

The best way to save money on meat is not to eat it. You'll not only save money but also your health. *Today's Health,* the magazine of the American Medical Association says:

> The average American has been conditioned to believe that only a meat-based diet can provide the nutrition necessary for good health. Traditionally, we are a nation of carnivores, consuming some fifteen pounds of meat per month. (The Japanese, by contrast, eat only about a half-pound, per person, per month.) Does this great U.S. "meat gorge" make nutritional sense? *Is* meat necessary to our health?[1]

Apparently, it is not; but its *protein* is. But when we consume a great amount of meat simply to get protein, we get more than we asked for:

> . . . The primary problem most American meat eaters face is not a deficiency of protein (most of us get all we need, and then some), but an excess of calories, because the meat we eat is so larded with saturated fat.

The fat not only adds to the meat for which we pay dearly but also adds unwelcome and dangerous weight to us:

> Most meat eaters . . . consistently exceed their limits in calories and, as a consequence, tend to weigh more. "Forty per cent of the fat in our diets comes from meat," says Dr. Frederick Star, chairman of the department of nutrition at the Harvard School of Public Health. "This fat is heavily—about 40 per cent— of the saturated, cholesterol-producing variety."

---

1. "Do We Eat Too Much Meat?", *Today's Health,* October, 1974, pp. 195, 197, 198.

Overall, meat is the most expensive way to eat protein. That doesn't mean you have to vow to become a vegetarian; it means you should buy and prepare meat stingily.

Here are a few ways to stretch your money on beef, chicken and fish.

Beef: You already know that the cheapest beef product is hamburger. You should also knowing the following:

Don't buy "hamburger-helping," "skillet-mix" dishes to go with hamburger. You can buy ingredients in the mixes separately and fix your own hamburger dishes.

Buy hamburger marked TVP (textured vegetable protein). You ought to know about TVP:

> Textured vegetable proteins are manufactured from defatted soybean flour or meal by a complicated process of spinning or extrusion that gives them a fibrous texture similar to cooked meat. They come in granules, bits, dices and chunks and in beef, ham and chicken flavors or unflavored. High in protein, they have no cholesterol, and little, if any, fat.[2]

Not only does TVP add body and appearance to hamburger but it also trims hamburger's price. One supermarket describes how TVP trims hamburger's price:

> By combining one pound of 75% lean ground beef with two-thirds cup of TVP, you wind up with 23 ounces of combined mixture at a cost of 72 cents a pound versus 93 cents for ground beef alone, a saving of 22%. When ground beef sells for $1.19 a pound, the difference between beef and beef plus soy protein climbs to 29¢, for a saving of 24%.

The cheapest way to prepare hamburger is in casseroles and meat loaves (recipes for both are in the recipe section). Make several casseroles and meat loaves at a time and freeze. That's cheaper *and easier* in the long run.

---

2. "Now There's Meatless Meat," *Changing Times*, February, 1974, pp. 53, 54.

If you are really aggressive about saving money on beef, and you have a freezer, look into buying a side of beef. The cost per pound includes steak, brisket, roasts, and filet as well as stew meat and hamburger. Obviously, you can't get steak and roasts, etc., for anything near the price of hamburger at your supermarket.

Poultry: Turkey, off season, is worth looking into. Whole chickens are cheaper than cut-up chickens. Buy several on sale and freeze. Chickens can be bought directly from area farmers who would be delighted to show an adventurous city-dweller how to kill, pluck, and dress a chicken.

Fish: If you live near the Atlantic or Pacific coast, go directly to the docks and buy fish as they are brought in. It is much cheaper and fresher that way. Of course, you can also get out and fish yourself. There are a lot of books and old salts who will tell you how to do that. I can't. I'm not a fisherman.

Vegetables and Fruits (Produce)

Grow your own vegetables and fruit. If you have the patience and sweat, a vegetable garden and fruit trees will pay for themselves over and over. A 20 x 30 garden plot—not much larger than many living rooms—yields 400 pounds of potatoes in a year.

If you can't grow your own, pick your own. Watch the newspapers and drive to adjacent rural areas asking local farmers where you can pick fruits and vegetables directly. It saves farmers the work and expense of picking, cleaning, hauling and selling. They'll probably charge a low fee. Strawberry farmers, for example, may charge 25¢ a basket if you come and pick your own. A similar basket in the supermarket costs three times as much.

Whether you grow or pick your own, you will need to learn how to properly can and freeze produce. The United States Department of Agriculture puts out several helpful books on canning, freezing, pickle and jelly-making. Write: Office of Communications, U.S.D.A., Washington, D.C. 20250.

Produce in the supermarket: Buy lower grade canned goods. Grade A is fancy, B is choice, C is standard. Buy grade C. Grades are based on color, texture, flavor, shape, uniformity, and freedom from defects—not on nutritional content.

Buy in-season fresh vegetables and fruits when available, rather than canned.

Finally . . .

Give money and food away to those who need it more than you. That's right. Part of the frustration and humiliation of living on tight wages is the lack of power and joy involved in helping others. Joy is always in giving, not in getting. Poor families, unfortunately, usually are robbed of that joy. They don't have to be.

Sounds impractical, doesn't it? But it works because God put this law in our universe: whatever *you* need, give it away.

Depressed and in need of encouragement? Give encouragement to someone else; *your* depression will vanish. Lonely and alone? Be a friend to another who is lonely; your loneliness will melt. Poor and worried? Give money to one poorer than yourself; your worry—and poverty—will fade. It's a joy and power not understood until tried.

The Psalmist said: "I have been young, and now am old; yet have I not seen the righteous forsaken, nor his children begging bread" (Ps. 37:25). He was right.

Editor's Note: More detailed information on saving money on food and other items, may be found in Neil Gallagher's recently published book, *How to Save Money on Almost Everything*, Bethany Fellowship, Inc., 1978.

ONE-DISH
WONDERS

MEAT CASSEROLES/SKILLET DINNERS

Ground Beef Casserole

Serve with salad and garlic bread for a complete meal.

1 lb. ground beef
1 medium onion chopped
Salt and pepper to taste
$\frac{1}{2}$ tsp. garlic powder
1 tsp. Worcestershire
$\frac{1}{2}$ tsp. oregano

1 can stewed tomatoes
Grated cheese
1 small pkg. large-shell
   macaroni

Brown meat with onion until done, but not hard. Add all seasonings and tomatoes. Simmer about 10 minutes. At the time you add the tomatoes and seasonings start boiling water for the macaroni and cook as is directed on package. Drain macaroni and add to meat mixture. Pour complete mixture into casserole and sprinkle grated cheese on top. Bake at 350° for about 30 minutes or until cheese is well melted.

Serves 6

Hamburger-Potato Bake

1 lb. hamburger
2 lbs. potatoes
2 cans cream of chicken soup
Salt and pepper to taste
Onion to taste

Brown hamburger in skillet. In separate skillet, lightly brown potatoes, "home-fries" fashion. Place hamburger, potatoes, and onions in layers in casserole dish or Dutch oven. Pour soup over entire mixture. Bake at 300° for 30 minutes or until mixture is boiling and potatoes are soft. (More potatoes and soup may be added to stretch out servings.)

Serves 6-8

Spanish Casserole

Serve with Harvard beets and apple crunch.

Lightly brown 1½ pounds ground beef with 1 chopped onion. Add 1 can (16 ounces) tomatoes (mashed), 1 can (12 ounces) corn (undrained), 1 can (8 ounces) tomato sauce, 2 teaspoons salt, ½ teaspoon pepper and 2 teaspoons chili powder. Cook 30 minutes over low heat. Add ½ cup yellow cornmeal and mix well. Put in shallow 2-quart baking dish. (If too dry, add a small amount of water.) Bake in preheated 350°-oven 45 minutes, or until lightly browned on top.

Serves 6

Southern Burger and Egg Casserole

4 hard-cooked eggs
4 T. butter, melted
¼ cup sifted all-purpose flour
½ tsp. salt
Dash pepper
2 cups milk

1 lb. hamburger, cooked and drained
1 can (16 oz.) whole-kernel corn, drained
1 cup soft bread crumbs (1½ slices)

Slice 2 of the eggs into 1½ quart casserole. In saucepan, blend butter, flour, salt, and pepper. Add milk all at once. Cook, stirring constantly, till mixture is boiling and thickened. Stir in hamburger and corn. Pour over sliced eggs. Slice remaining 2 eggs; arrange over top of hamburger mixture. Sprinkle with bread crumbs. Bake at 375° for 20 to 25 minutes or till heated through.

Serves 6

Pigs in the Blanket

Break off 8 cabbage leaves and boil about two minutes. Boil ¾ cup rice until almost soft. Brown ½ pound hamburger. Mix hamburger and rice, then roll 2 tablespoons of mixture in cabbage leaf. Put in greased pan with small amount of water. Add tomato soup, and cover. Bake 45 minutes at 350°. Add more water and bake 20 minutes longer.

Serves 4

Tamale Pie Casserole

Good on cold days!

¾ lb. hamburger
¾ lb. ground pork
½ cup onion, chopped
½ cup green pepper
1 can tomatoes
2 tsp. chili powder

2 tsp. salt
½ tsp. black pepper
Corn meal mush (see
   directions on corn meal
   package)
1 cup grated cheese

Brown meat, onion, and green pepper—add tomatoes, chili powder, salt and pepper. Simmer 20 minutes. Line bottom and sides of 2-quart casserole with mush, saving one cup to spread on top. Pour in hot meat mixture. Top with remaining mush. Bake one hour in moderate oven (375°). Last 15 minutes, spread on cheese.

Serves 8

Barbecued Burger 'n Beans

1 cup dried red or pink beans
   (about 3 cups cooked)
3 cups water
1 tsp. salt
1 lb. hamburger
½ cup chopped onion
1 T. oil
1 cup catsup
¼ cup cider vinegar

1 T. brown sugar
1 tsp. salt
⅛ tsp. pepper
½ tsp. chili powder
1 tsp. Worcestershire sauce
Hamburger buns, toasted and
   buttered
Onion rings for garnish

Soak beans in water overnight. Cook beans in soaking water, with the addition of 1 teaspoon salt, until tender, about 2 hours. Drain. Saute hamburger and onion in oil. Add beans, catsup, vinegar, brown sugar, and seasonings.

Cover and simmer 15 to 20 minutes. Serve over toasted and buttered hamburger buns. Garnish with onion rings if you like.

Serves 6-8

Quick Spanish Beef-Rice

1/4 cup vegetable oil
1 medium onion, thinly sliced
1/2 medium green pepper, chopped
1/2 lb. hamburger
1 cup regular rice, uncooked

2 (8-oz.) cans tomato sauce
1 3/4 cups hot water
1 tsp. salt
Dash pepper
1 tsp. prepared mustard

Heat oil in skillet. Add onion, green pepper, hamburger and rice. Stir over high heat until lightly browned. Add tomato sauce and remaining ingredients. Mix well. Bring quickly to a boil. Cover tightly, and simmer 25 minutes. Meat may be omitted; 1/2 cup grated cheese may be added if desired just before serving time.

Serves 4

One-Skillet Corned Beef Dinner

2 T. butter or margarine
6 small boiled potatoes
1/8 tsp. salt
1/8 tsp. pepper
1 (12-oz.) can corned beef, cut into 4 slices

1 (16-oz.) can sauerkraut, drained
2 cups boiled carrot slices
2 tsp. prepared horseradish
2 tsp. prepared mustard

Melt butter in a 10-inch skillet over moderately low heat (about 225°). Add potatoes, sprinkle with salt and pepper and turn up heat to moderately high (about 300°); cook potatoes 5 to 7 minutes, turning frequently, until outsides are crisp and lightly browned. Push potatoes to one side of skillet. Add corned beef to skillet and cook until brown and crisp on both sides. Remove skillet from heat and add sauerkraut; keep separate and do not mix them with the potatoes or corned beef. Nestle the carrots in the sauerkraut. Reduce heat to moderate (about 250°); cover skillet and cook 10 minutes until sauerkraut and carrots are warmed through. Meanwhile, mix horseradish and mustard separately. Serve from skillet or transfer to a heated serving dish. Serve sauce separately.

Serves 4

All-in-One Blender Dinner

Blend until coarsely grated:
2 medium onions, cut up
1/2 clove garlic, cut
1/2 green pepper, diced

Cook in boiling, salted water, 1/4 pound medium noodles. Drain. Stir in 1 tablespoon butter. Heat 2 tablespoons oil in large skillet. Add 1 pound hamburger. Pour into skillet blended vegetables from container. Brown lightly. Season well with salt and pepper. Add cooked noodles, 1 can drained corn and 2 cups stewed tomatoes. Stir and heat gently. Place in container 1/4 pound diced American cheese and 1 slice broken bread. Cover and blend about 30 seconds. Sprinkle crumbs over skillet, and broil 2 minutes until brown.

Serves 6

Spanish Hamburger

Serve with rice and a vegetable.

Cook three onions (chopped fine) in small amount of water for 5 minutes. Don't drain off water. Add:

2½ lbs. hamburger	2½ tsp. salt
3 T. mustard	¼ tsp. pepper
2 T. chili powder	

Cook 1½ hours uncovered on low heat.

Serves 8

Burger 'n Bean Surprise

2 cups cooked pinto beans	1 tsp. chili powder
1 lb. hamburger	2 cups tomato juice
1 large onion, chopped	Pinch cumin seed or powder
1 clove garlic	Salt and pepper to taste

Brown meat and add onion; cook until onion is tender; add garlic and other ingredients. Simmer 1 to 1½ hours.

Serves 6

Hamburger Supreme

Brown in large skillet over medium heat 1 pound hamburger. Add ½ cup chopped onion, and cool. Stir in:

¾ cup milk
1 pkg. (8 oz.) cream cheese
1 can (10½-oz.) condensed cream of mushroom soup
1½ cups whole-kernel corn

¼ cup chopped pimiento
1 pkg. (8-oz.) noodles, cooked and drained
1 tsp. salt
Dash pepper

Simmer over low heat until thoroughly hot.

Serves 8

Beef-Potato Boats

All-in-one meat and potato meal. Easy!

Bake 4 medium-size potatoes. Meanwhile, lightly brown 1 pound hamburger, ½ cup chopped celery and 1 small chopped onion in skillet. Drain fat. Add 1 teaspoon salt, ¼ teaspoon nutmeg, 1 (8-oz.) can Tomato Sauce with Onions. Cut potatoes in half lengthwise; scoop out and reserve shells. Mash potatoes, combine with meat mixture. Fill shells; place in baking pan. Sprinkle 1 cup shredded Cheddar cheese on top. Bake 15 minutes at 400°.

Serves 4

Spoon Burgers

A tasty Sloppy Joe.

4 T. oil
1 medium onion, chopped
1 lb. hamburger
1 tsp. salt
½ cup catsup

2 T. prepared mustard
3 T. barbecue sauce
3 T. Worcestershire sauce

Brown ground beef and onions in oil. Add other ingredients and let simmer for five minutes. Spoon over hamburger buns and serve hot.

Serves 4

Corned Beef Hash

1 T. butter or margarine
1 (16 oz.) can corned beef hash
1/3 cup chopped, peeled onion
1/8 tsp pepper

1 (16-oz.) jar sliced pickled beets, drained and cut into strips
3 T. very coarsely chopped sweet mixed pickles

Melt butter in a heavy, 10-inch skillet over moderate heat (about 250°). In a medium-sized bowl mix the hash with the onion and pepper. Transfer hash to the heated skillet and press down firmly with a pancake turner. Cook hash for 13 to 15 minutes, turning it when it browns on the bottom. Reduce heat if hash sticks; increase heat slightly if hash does not seem to be browning. When most of the hash is nicely browned, stir in the beets and pickles and cook about 3 minutes longer, turning the mixture frequently.

Serves 4

Meat 'n Macaroni Supper

1 medium onion, chopped
2 T. butter, melted
1 (8-oz.) can tomatoes, cut up
1/4 teaspoon thyme
Dash pepper
1 can condensed cream of celery soup

1/2 (7-oz.) pkg. elbow macaroni, cooked and drained
1 (12-oz.) can luncheon meat, cut in 1 x 1 1/2-inch strips
1/4 cup chopped green pepper
1/4 cup shredded American cheese

In medium skillet, cook onion in butter or margarine till tender but not brown. Stir in the soup, tomatoes, thyme, and pepper. Add the cooked macaroni, luncheon meat, and green pepper. Spoon into 1 1/2-quart casserole. Top with shredded cheese. Bake, uncovered, in moderate oven (350°) for 35 to 40 minutes or till heated through.

Serves 4-6

Budget Dinner in a Skillet

Brown 1 pound ground beef with 3 stalks celery, cut in diagonal slices, and 1 medium onion, cut in fairly coarse chunks. Add 2 cups leftover boiled potatoes, cut in bite-size pieces, and ½ cup leftover whole-kernel corn. Blend all with a thin white sauce and season with salt, pepper and a whiff of marjoram. Simmer slowly 10 to 15 minutes.

Suggestion: Since this is colorless, serve with Harvard beets and gelatin vegetable salad, milk and white cake with peach topping.

Serves 4

Beans 'n Hamburger

Applesauce is good with this.

Pour water (just to cover) over 1 pound pinto beans and soak overnight. In the morning, add water to about 1 inch over beans. Add 1 pound ground beef (broken up) and 1 large chopped onion. Simmer very gently until beans start to get tender. Add 1 can (16 ounces) tomatoes (mashed) and season with ½ teaspoon pepper, ¼ teaspoon marjoram, ¼ teaspoon garlic powder and salt to taste. Continue simmering until beans are done. Turn off heat and let stand 30 minutes to 1 hour. Reheat and serve with biscuits, corn bread or rolls.

Serves 6

ONE-DISH PORK WONDERS

Cheap Ham Casserole

Preheat oven to 400°

½ cup cooking oil
½ cup very small onions
1 small can mushrooms
¼ cup flour (pre-sifted)

1½ cup milk
1 can cream of celery soup
1 cup sharp cheese, grated
Dash black pepper
3 cups cooked cubed ham

Topping:

Mix 1½ cups dry biscuit mix with ½ cup grated cheese. Add ⅔ cup milk until ingredients are moistened. Add 2 tablespoons finely minced onion.

Sauté onions in oil. Add mushrooms and lower heat to simmer. Add flour, then milk, stirring well after each addition. Allow to thicken. Now add soup and cheese. Lower heat to simmer. Add pepper and ham. Remove from heat and pour into large baking dish. Add topping. Bake till topping is brown and done (a toothpick inserted into topping comes out clean.) About 20-30 minutes.

Serves 4-6

Frankfurter Noodle Casserole

Mix ½ cup each finely chopped green pepper and onion, 2 tablespoons prepared mustard and 1 tablespoon flour. Simmer 1⅔ cups undiluted canned milk and ½ teaspoon salt in saucepan over low heat to just below boiling. Add 2 cups (8 oz.) shredded American Cheese; stir over low heat until cheese melts. Place 3 cups cooked noodles in buttered 10 x 6-inch baking dish. Top with 1 pound frankfurters. Spread green pepper mixture over frankfurters. Pour cheese sauce over all. Bake in 350°-oven about 30 minutes.

Serves 6

Ham-Turkey Pie

4 T. butter or margarine
5 T. all-purpose flour
1/4 tsp. pepper
2 cups chicken broth
1 cup diced cooked ham

1 cup diced cooked turkey
1/2 cup sliced mushrooms
1/4 cup chopped green onion
3 T. snipped parsley
1 recipe for rice shell

In saucepan, melt butter or margarine; blend in flour and pepper. Add chicken broth all at once. Cook over medium heat, stirring constantly, till mixture thickens and bubbles. Add ham, turkey, mushrooms, onion, and parsley; mix thoroughly. Pour into prepared rice shell. Bake in 350° oven for 40 minutes. Let stand 5 to 8 minutes.

To make rice shell: Combine 2 1/2 cups cooked long-grain rice, 2 beaten eggs, 4 tablespoons melted butter, and 1/8 teaspoon pepper; mix thoroughly. Press firmly into an ungreased 9-inch pie plate.

Serves 6

Leftovers Casserole

4 eggs
1/2 cup milk
1/2 cup water

2 T. melted butter
1 cup flour
3/4 tsp. salt

Combine ingredients and let batter stand one hour. Meanwhile: Sauté one chopped onion in one tablespoon butter. Mix with 2 cups of any chopped, leftover meat such as ham, turkey, chicken, roast; or 2 cups ground beef that has been browned and drained; or 2 cups drained canned tuna. Add 1/4 cup chopped pimiento, salt and pepper to taste and just enough liquid to moisten mixture (either stock, milk or water). Preheat oven to 400°.

Heat an 8" skillet; brush with butter. Pour batter into pan by scant 1/4 cupfuls. Turn and tip pan so mixture covers most of bottom. Turn crepes after a few seconds and cook other side. Fill crepes with meat mixture and roll up. Place in shallow baking dish. Cover with 1 cup of your favorite cheese sauce (or use cheese soup). Bake at 400° until brown and bubbly.

Serves 6-8.

Sausage Casserole

1 lb. sausage
1 small onion, chopped
1 clove garlic, minced
½ cup chopped green pepper

1 can kidney beans
1 (8-oz.) can tomato sauce
1 tsp. oregano

Remove casing from sausage. Brown in electric skillet set at 375° (or over medium heat in regular skillet). Pour off fat.

Add onion, green pepper and garlic. Cook until soft. Add kidney beans, undrained; tomato sauce and oregano.

Cover; turn control to 220° (or turn burner to low) and simmer 30 minutes.

Serves 4

Ham and Sweet Potato Casserole

6 medium sweet potatoes or 1
   (1-lb.) can sweet potatoes
3 T. melted butter or
   margarine, divided
½ tsp. salt
⅛ tsp. pepper
Dash ground nutmeg
Milk

2 cups diced, cooked ham
1 (20-oz.) can pineapple
   chunks
½ cup green pepper, chopped
2 T. brown sugar
1 T. cornstarch
2 T. vinegar

Cook potatoes in small amount of water until tender. Cool and peel. (If using canned potatoes, drain off all the juice except for the very thick bottom syrup.) Mash well; add 1 tablespoon butter and the salt, pepper, nutmeg, and enough milk to whip potatoes to fluffy stage.

Sauté ham in 2 tablespoons butter until brown. Drain pineapple, reserving ¾ cup juice. Add green pepper and pineapple chunks to ham; cook 2 or 3 minutes. Combine brown sugar and cornstarch; stir into ham mixture. Add reserved pineapple juice and vinegar. Cook and stir until thick and clear. Pour ham mixture into a 3 or 4-quart baking dish. Drop tablespoonfuls of potatoes over ham mixture. Bake at 400° for 20 minutes or until bubbly.

Serves 6-8

Sausage Noodle Casserole

1 lb. sausage (or hamburger)
1 onion, chopped
1 green pepper, chopped
1 (20 oz.) can corn
1 (10-oz.) can mushroom soup

1 cup milk
1 cup grated cheese
1 pkg. noodles (cooked)

Brown the sausage in skillet until done. Add the onion, pepper, corn and soup. Now add the milk and cook together till blended well. Add the cheese and noodles and bake in casserole dish for 30 minutes at 350°.

Serves 6

Corn Bread and Bacon Casserole

5 to 6 slices bacon
1 cup diced celery
¼ cup chopped onion
3 cups coarse corn bread crumbs

3 slices bread, toasted and cubed
½ tsp. rubbed sage
1 cup chicken bouillon

Cook bacon till crisp. Drain, reserving ¼ cup of the drippings. Crumble bacon and set aside. Add (in same skillet) celery, onion, and ½ cup water. Cover and cook until vegetables are just tender (about 7 minutes). In large bowl, combine bacon, vegetable mixture and liquid, corn bread crumbs, toast cubes, sage, reserved ¼ cup bacon drippings and bouillon; toss well. Turn into 1½-quart casserole. Cover and bake in 350°-oven for 30 minutes.

Serves 4-6

Pork-Potato Casserole

Good use of leftover pork.

Slice a layer of potatoes into a casserole. Add a layer of sliced onions, then a layer of pork pieces. Repeat layers, ending with potatoes, and season each layer with salt and pepper as you go. Then pour milk to ½" from top. Bake in preheated 350°-oven 1 hour, or until potatoes are tender and well browned on top.

Sweet and Sour Weiners 'n Beans

1 cup dried red or pink beans
3 cups water
1 tsp. salt
1 lb. weiners
2 T. butter or margarine
1 small onion, sliced
1 green pepper, cut in strips
2 T. flour

1 (13¼ ozs.) can pineapple
   chunks
½ cup water
1 (8-oz.) can tomato sauce
1 beef bouillon cube
¼ tsp. salt
2 T. sugar
2 T. lemon juice
1 T. soy sauce

Soak beans in water overnight. Cook beans in soaking water, with addition of 1 teaspoon salt, until tender, about 2 hours. Drain, Score weiners, making shallow (¼-inch) diagonal cuts, 1 inch apart. Brown slightly in butter and remove from pan.

Saute onion and green pepper in remaining butter. Blend in flour. Drain pineapple, reserving syrup. Add pineapple syrup, water, tomato sauce, and bouillon cube to skillet.

Cook, stirring, until bouillon cube is dissolved and sauce is smooth. Add beans, salt, sugar, lemon juice, and soy sauce.

Cover and simmer 10 minutes. Add pineapple and weiners and simmer just until heated through.

Serves 6

Spam Italiana

1 (12-oz.) can Spam
Mozzarella cheese
1 cup catsup (or tomato sauce, 8-oz. can)
½ tsp. oregano
Dash garlic powder

Preheat oven to 400°. Place Spam in pie pan. Cut into five equal slices. Cut cheese to fit between Spam slices. Hold together with toothpicks. Mix the rest of the ingredients together, pour over the top. Bake 20 minutes.

Serves 5

Bologna-Vegetable Dinner

4 large potatoes, peeled and
   cut in ½-in. slices
1 to 2 cups sliced carrots
1 small head cabbage, cut
   in quarters and sliced
   lengthwise in 1-in. strips
1 (8-oz.) can tomato sauce

2 tsp. salt
2 tsp. whole cumin seed
¼ tsp. black pepper
1½ lb. bologna, cut in
   ½-in. slices
Chopped parsley
Prepared mustard

Layer potatoes in large heavy saucepan. Add next 6 ingredients
and 1 cup water. Bring to boil, reduce heat, cover and simmer 20
minutes. Put bologna on top of cabbage, cover and simmer 6 to 8
minutes. Sprinkle generously with parsley and serve with mustard.

Serves 6

Frank-Vegetable Medley

½ lb. frankfurters, cut in 1-inch
   pieces
½ cup long-grain rice
1 (8-oz.) can tomato sauce
1 cup water

1 (10-oz.) pkg, frozen mixed
   vegetables, slightly thawed
¼ cup chopped onion
1 tsp. salt
Dash bottled hot pepper sauce

Combine ingredients in 2-quart casserole. Bake, covered, in 375°-
oven for 1 hour or until heated through. Stir once or twice during
baking time.

Serves 6

Franks and Beans Skillet Supper

2 slices bacon
6 franks
½ cup chopped onion
1 can cream of chicken soup

½ cup water
3 cups sliced cooked potatoes
1 cup cooked, cut green beans
⅛ tsp. leaf thyme, crushed

In skillet, fry bacon; remove and crumble. Cut each frank into
thirds. In drippings, brown franks and cook onion until tender. Stir
in soup, water, potatoes, green beans and thyme. Heat, stir,
garnish with bacon.

Serves 4

Pork and Vegetable Rice Dinner

1 lb. boneless pork, cut into 1-inch cubes
2 T. butter or margarine
¼ cup sliced green onion
2 cups water
1½ tsp. salt

1 cup uncooked rice (not instant)
1 chicken bouillon cube
⅛ tsp. pepper
1 (10-oz.) pkg. frozen Brussels sprouts, cooked and drained (about 2 cups)
1 cup cooked sliced carrots

Brown pork cubes well on all sides in butter or margarine in heavy frying pan over moderate heat. Add onion, ¼ cup water and ½ teaspoon salt. Cover and cook over low heat 30 minutes. Add remaining 1¾ cups water, rice, bouillon cube, 1 teaspoon salt and pepper; mix. Cover; cook over low heat until pork is tender, about 30 minutes. Add vegetables; mix carefully, cover and heat 3 to 4 minutes. Serve with fruit sauce.

Serves 4

Fruit Sauce:

1 (10-oz.) jar tart apple or currant jelly
⅓ cup catsup
¼ cup water

3 T. lemon juice
¾ tsp. prepared mustard
⅛ tsp. ground cloves
¼ tsp. salt

Combine ingredients in heavy saucepan. Heat to simmering and cook slowly until jelly melts and flavors blend, 3 to 4 minutes.

Makes about 1¾ cups sauce.

HAMBURGER PIES AND MEAT LOAVES

Hamburger Pie

Tasty and economical

1 onion, finely chopped
1 lb. hamburger
1 can green beans
1 egg

1 can tomato soup
Salt and pepper to taste
6 or 7 cooked potatoes

Brown onion in small amount of shortening, add ground beef and cook slowly until done, then add drained green beans, tomato soup; let simmer about 10 minutes. Cream potatoes, add raw egg to potatoes and beat thoroughly. Put meat mixture in a casserole, top with creamed potatoes, put in 375°-oven until brown.

Serves 6

Cottage Pie

Sauté 1 onion (chopped) and 1 clove garlic (crushed) in 2 T. oil until soft. Add 1 pound hamburger, 2 carrots (grated), 1 stalk celery (chopped). Cover and simmer until meat is done. Remove from heat. Make mashed potatoes. Put hamburger mixture in casserole and pile potatoes on top. Sprinkle Parmesan cheese on top and place in oven until browned.

Serves 4-6

Souper Meat 'n Potatoes Pie

1 can cream of mushroom
    soup
1 lb. hamburger
¼ cup finely chopped onion
1 egg, slightly beaten

¼ cup fine dry bread crumbs
2 T. chopped parsley
¼ tsp. salt
Dash pepper
2 cups mashed potatoes
¼ cup shredded mild cheese

Mix thoroughly ½ cup soup, beef, onion, egg, bread crumbs, parsley, and seasonings. Press firmly into 9-inch pie plate. Bake at 350° for 25 minutes; spoon off fat. Frost with potatoes; top with remaining soup and cheese. Bake 10 minutes more or until done. Garnish with cooked sliced bacon if desired.

Serves 6

Beef 'n Biscuit Pie

1 lb. hamburger	1 tsp. chili powder
½ cup chopped onion	2 cups biscuit mix
1 (8-oz.) can tomato sauce	⅔ cup milk
1 tsp. salt	¼ cup vegetable oil

Brown hamburger in skillet. Add onion; cook until tender; drain fat. Add sauce, salt, chili powder; heat. Combine biscuit mix, milk, oil. Knead on floured board. Pat half the dough in 9-inch pie pan. Pour in hot filling.

Pat out remaining dough and place over filling. Crimp edge; slit top. Bake at 425° for 20-25 minutes.

Serves 4-6

Chili Loaf

1 lb. hamburger	2 cups cornmeal
1 lb. sausage	1 cup milk
1 (16-oz.) can tomatoes	2 eggs
1 (16-oz.) can creamed corn	2 tsp. salt
1 cup onion, chopped	2 T. chili powder
Catsup to taste	1 T. margarine

Cook beef and sausage until crumbly. Add tomatoes, corn, and onion. Cook over medium heat 10 minutes. Combine cornmeal, milk, eggs, salt, chili powder, and margarine, add to meat. Pour into 2-qt. casserole. Bake 1 hour in moderate oven, 350°. Top with catsup.

Serves 12

Sweet-and-Sour Meat Loaf

1 (15-oz.) can tomato sauce
½ cup light brown sugar, firmly
    packed
¼ cup vinegar
1 tsp. prepared mustard
2 lbs. hamburger

½ lb. ground pork
2 eggs, slightly beaten
½ cup minced onion
½ cup soft bread crumbs
2 tsp. salt
¼ tsp. pepper

Combine tomato sauce, brown sugar, vinegar and mustard. Combine meat, eggs, onion, bread crumbs, and seasonings; add 1 cup tomato sauce mixture. Pack into a 1½-quart casserole dish. Pour ¼ cup sauce over meat loaf. Bake at 350° for 1 hour. Heat remaining sauce and serve with meat loaf.

Serves 6

Meat Loaf

2 lbs. hamburger
1 cup rolled oats
1 beaten egg

1 chopped onion
2 tsp. salt
¼ tsp. pepper
¾ cup milk

Mix thoroughly. Form into loaf in large heavy skillet or baking pan and bake in preheated 350°-oven 1 hour. When done, gently remove from skillet to a serving plate and let stand 5 minutes before slicing.

For gravy, to use for another meal; put skillet on top of the range. Add 2 cups water to the drippings, stir well and bring to boil. In a pint jar with tight-fitting lid, put 2 to 3 T. flour and 1 cup water. Shake well until smooth, then slowly pour from the jar into the skillet, stirring constantly, until the gravy thickens. Reduce heat and simmer 5 minutes, then season with salt, pepper and a whiff of marjoram. Have baked potatoes with the meat loaf this time; use the gravy with leftover meat loaf later in the week, either in hot meat loaf sandwiches or over noodles.

Serves 8

Meat Loaf II

Combine 1½ pounds hamburger with ¾ cup uncooked rolled oats, ¾ cup milk, 1 chopped onion, ½ teaspoon salt and ¼ teaspoon pepper. Shape into loaf and bake in preheated 350°-oven 45 minutes. Beat ½ cup any kind of jelly and blend in 1 tablespoon dry mustard and 1 tablespoon brown sugar. Spread jelly mixture over top of meat loaf and bake 15 minutes longer.

Serves 6

Favorite Beef Loaf

1½ lbs. hamburger	2 T. chopped green pepper
½ cup medium cracker crumbs	Dash thyme
2 beaten eggs	Dash marjoram
1 (8-oz.) can tomato sauce	1 tsp. salt
¼ cup finely chopped onion	

Combine all ingredients; mix well. Shape mixture into a loaf in a 12 x 7 x 2-inch baking dish. Bake in a 350°-oven 1¼-1½ hours.

Serves 6-8

Stuffed Meat Loaf

1 lb. hamburger	2 eggs
½ cup chopped green pepper	¼ cup oil
½ cup chopped onion	2 cups whole-wheat bread
1 tsp. salt	crumbs
1 T. Worcestershire sauce	½ cup chopped celery
1 cup white bread, broken into	¼ tsp. black pepper
small pieces	¾ cup meat stock
½ cup milk	Nuts (optional)

Combine hamburger, green pepper, onion, salt, Worcestershire sauce, white bread, milk and one egg. Mix. Place half of mixture in bottom of greased loaf pan. Combine remaining ingredients and spread on top of meat mixture. Arrange remaining meat mixture on top of stuffing. Bake at 350° for 1½ hours.

Serves 4-6

Tomato Meat Loaf

1 can tomato soup
2 lbs. hamburger
½ cup fine, dry bread crumbs
½ cup chopped parsley

1 T. Worcestershire sauce
1 egg, slightly beaten
1 tsp. salt

Mix all ingredients thoroughly. Shape firmly into loaf, place in shallow baking pan. Bake at 350° about 1¼ hours.

Serves 8

20-Minute Meat Loaves

1½ lbs. hamburger
1 tsp. salt
⅛ tsp. pepper
1 T. grated onion

1 egg
½ cup quick-cooking oats
½ cup catsup

Shape into 8 oval loaves. Place in baking dish. Bake at 450° for 20 minutes. Serve topped with more catsup.

Serves 4-5

Filled Meat Loaf

Combine thoroughly:

1½ lbs. hamburger
¾ cup rolled oats
1 egg, beaten
1 cup tomato juice

¼ cup chopped onion
1½ tsp. salt
¼ tsp. pepper

Heat in saucepan over medium heat 2 tablespoons margarine. Add ½ cup chopped onion and cook until lightly browned. Remove from heat. Stir in 1 cup cooked vegetables: sliced green beans, diced carrots, diced potatoes or mixed vegetables.

Firmly pack half of meat mixture into loaf pan. Make a shallow "well" lengthwise down center of meat mixture. Spoon vegetable mixture into "well." Shape remaining meat mixture over vegetables being careful to cover all. Seal edges. Bake in moderate oven (350°) 1 hour and 10 minutes. Remove from oven and let stand 5 minutes before slicing.

Serves 8

Quick Onion-Mushroom Meat Loaf

1¼ lb. hamburger
1 cup cracker crumbs or
    oatmeal
½ envelope onion soup mix

½ envelope mushroom soup
    mix
1 can vegetable soup
1 egg
1 tsp. salt

Mix ingredients, place in loaf pan and bake at 350° about 1 hour.

Serves 4

Cheese-Filled Meat Loaf

1½ lbs. hamburger
1 cup tomato sauce
1 egg
½ cup dry bread crumbs

¼ cup chopped onion
1 tsp. salt
¼ tsp. thyme

Combine and pack half of mixture into loaf pan. Arrange 4 slices cheese on top. Pack remaining meat over cheese. Turn out into shallow pan. Bake at 350° for 40 minutes. Remove excess fat. Pour 1 cup tomato sauce over mixture. Bake 30 minutes longer.

Serves 5-6

Topnotch Turkey Loaf

4 cups coarsely ground, cooked
    turkey
1½ cups soft bread crumbs
1 (6-oz.) can (⅔ cup)
    evaporated milk
⅓ cup chicken broth

⅔ cup finely chopped celery
2 slightly beaten eggs
¾ tsp. salt
Dash each: pepper, ground
    nutmeg, dried rosemary
    and dried marjoram, crushed

Lightly combine all ingredients. Line bottom of greased 8½ x 4½ x 2½-inch loaf dish with foil; grease foil. Turn in turkey mixture. Bake in 350°-oven for 45 minutes, until center of loaf is firm. Invert onto serving platter; remove foil.

Serve with Pimiento Sauce: Heat together 1 can condensed cream of chicken soup, ⅓ cup milk, and 2 tablespoons chopped pimiento.

Serves 6

TUNA/SALMON DISHES

Tuna 'n Chips Casserole

1 can cream of mushroom
    soup
1/2 cup milk

1 can flaked tuna fish
1 cup peas
1 cup crushed potato chips

Mix in a 2-quart casserole dish. Top with 1/4 cup crushed potato chips. Bake in 350°-oven for 30 minutes. For variation, substitute lima beans for peas and add a little onion salt.

Serves 4-6

Tuna Dinner-Cakes

1 1/2 cups sifted all-purpose flour
1/2 tsp. salt
1/2 cup shortening
1/2 cup shredded, sharp
    Cheddar cheese
4 T. water
1/4 cup shortening
1/4 cup chopped onion

1/4 cup thinly sliced celery
1/4 cup flour
1 3/4 cups flour
2 cans (6 1/2 or 7-oz.) tuna,
    drained
1 tsp. salt
Dash pepper

Combine 1 1/2 cups flour and 1/2 teaspoon salt in bowl. Cut in 1/2 cup shortening and cheese until uniform but coarse. Sprinkle with water, toss with fork and press into a ball. On lightly floured surface, roll out pastry about 1/8-inch thick. Cut out twelve pastry circles, 3 inches in diameter. Place on ungreased baking sheet in 425° oven about 15 minutes, or until lightly browned.

    Meanwhile, melt 1/4 cup shortening in medium saucepan. Stir in onion and celery. Cook until almost tender. Stir in 1/4 cup flour. Gradually add milk; cook and stir over medium heat until sauce boils 2 minutes. Stir in tuna, salt and pepper. Heat thoroughly. Using 2 pastry rounds for each serving, layer with spoonfuls of tuna mixture.

Serves 6

Tuna Loaf

1 envelope (1 T.) unflavored gelatin
1 cup cold water, divided
½ tsp. salt
¼ tsp. celery salt
1 T. lemon juice
Dash pepper or paprika
½ cup mayonnaise
½ cup chopped celery
3 T. chopped sweet pickle or olives
1 (6½-oz) can tuna, drained and flaked
Lettuce
Cucumber slices (optional)
Tomato slices (optional)

Sprinkle gelatin in ½ cup water in a small saucepan; set aside for 5 minutes. Place over medium heat, and stir until gelatin is dissolved; blend in remaining ½ cup water, salt, celery salt, lemon juice, pepper, and mayonnaise.

Combine celery, pickle, tuna, and gelatin mixture. Pour into a greased 9-inch loaf pan, and chill until firm. Unmold on lettuce, and garnish with cucumber and tomato slices if desired.

Serves 6

Tuna Loaf II

Left over tuna loaf makes delicious sandwiches.

2 eggs
½ cup mayonnaise or salad dressing
1 medium size onion finely chopped
½ pkg. corn bread stuffing (or make your own corn bread, crumble, and use for stuffing)
2-oz. jar of sliced pimientos and liquid
1 can mushroom soup
2 (6½-oz.) cans chunk-style tuna

Beat eggs. Add salad dressing, onion, corn bread stuffing, pimientos and soup; mix well. Stir in flaked tuna with the oil. Put in oblong baking dish. Bake in 375°-oven about 1 hour, or until firm. To vary the loaf, use celery soup or soup of your choice.

Serves 6-8

Tuna Casserole Supper

3 large carrots, sliced
1 box french-cut green beans
1 can cream of chicken soup

1 (8-oz.) pkg. noodles (cooked)
2 small cans chunk tuna
½ cup small cheese crackers,
    crushed

Put carrot slices into ¾ cup boiling salted water. Cook for 5 minutes, add box of beans which have been partially thawed and cook an additional 5 minutes. Season with butter and onion salt. Combine (along with their liquid) very lightly with next three ingredients in greased 2-quart casserole. Sprinkle cracker crumbs over top and bake 25 minutes at 325°.

Serves 6

Tuna Tetrizoni

4 oz. cooked spaghetti
2 cans of tuna fish
½ cup green peppers, chopped
¼ cup pimientos
1 small onion, chopped fine

½ cup water
1 can mushroom soup
1¾ cup sharp Cheddar cheese
    (reserve ½ for topping)

Cook spaghetti in boiling water with salt, drain; add tuna, pimientos, pepper, onions, water, mushroom soup and cheese. Put in baking dish (greased) and bake 45 minutes at 350°. The last 5 minutes, sprinkle remainder of cheese over the top and put back into oven to melt.

Serves 8

Tuna-Mix Casserole

2½ cups shredded carrot
1 cup finely chopped onion
1½ cups chopped celery
1 green pepper, chopped
2½ cups chopped, raw escarole
    or spinach

2 (6½- or 7-oz.) cans tuna,
    drained and flaked
2 cups cooked rice
¼ cup wheat germ
3 eggs, beaten
2 T. shredded Cheddar cheese

Place carrot, onion, celery, and green pepper in a colander over boiling water. Cover; steam until barely tender. Add escarole or spinach, and steam an additional 3 minutes. Place vegetables in a bowl and add remaining ingredients. Mix well. Spoon mixture into a greased 3-quart baking dish. Cover; bake at 350° for 30 minutes.

Serves 8

Salmon-Egg Casserole

1 (16 oz.) can salmon	1 cup light cream
2 T. lemon juice	1/2 tsp. salt
4 hard-cooked eggs, sliced	1/4 tsp. Tabasco sauce
1 cup cooked or canned green beans	1 tsp. Worcestershire sauce
4 T. butter	1 cup grated, sharp Cheddar cheese
3 T. flour	1 cup soft bread crumbs

Drain salmon, reserve liquid. Flake salmon, keeping pieces fairly large; sprinkle with lemon juice. Arrange salmon, eggs and green beans in alternate layers in greased 1½-quart casserole. Melt 3 tablespoons of the butter. Add flour; stir to a smooth paste. Measure salmon liquid, adding enough water, if necessary, to make ½ cup; combine with cream; add to flour mixture. Cook, stirring constantly, until mixture thickens and comes to a boil. Add salt, Tabasco, Worcestershire sauce and cheese; stir until cheese is melted. Pour into casserole. Add remaining 1 tablespoon melted butter to bread crumbs; sprinkle over top. Bake in 375°-oven about 30 minutes, or until crumbs are golden brown. Serve with pickles, relish, or with crisp salad and crackers.

Serves 4

Salmon Loaf I

1 (16 oz.) can salmon	1 tsp. baking powder
3 T. melted butter	1 tsp. lemon juice
1 cup fine bread crumbs	½ cup celery, chopped
1 cup scalded milk	2 beaten egg yolks
1 tsp. salt	2 beaten egg whites

Preheat oven to 350°. Combine all ingredients except egg whites and mix well. Fold stiffly beaten egg whites into mixture. *Steam bake 60 minutes. Unmold on serving plate. Serve with crisp salad.

Serves 8

*Steam-bake is the process often used in the preparation of bread pudding. The mixture (whatever it is) is placed in a pan and *that* pan is placed in a pan of water in the oven.

Salmon Loaf II

Drain (reserving liquid) 1 (16 oz.) can salmon. Combine drained, flaked salmon with the following (mixing well):

3 cups fine bread cubes	Dash cayenne
1½ T. chopped parsley	½ tsp. celery salt
1 T. lemon juice	2 grated onion
1¼ tsp. salt	3 butter

Place in greased 9 x 5 x 3-inch pan. Combine 2 eggs, well beaten, and the salmon liquid plus milk to make ¾ cup. Pour liquid mixture over salmon mixture in pan. Bake in 350°-oven for 45 minutes or until loaf is firm in center.

Serves 6

Salmon a la Vegetables

1 (16-oz.) can salmon
1/4 cup chopped onion
1/4 cup melted margarine
1/4 cup flour
1/2 tsp. salt

Pepper to taste
2 cups milk
1 (8½-oz.) can peas and
    carrots, undrained

Drain liquid from salmon; reserve liquid. Break salmon into large pieces. Saute onion in margarine until soft; stir in flour, salt, and pepper. Add milk a little at a time; stir constantly until mixture is thick. Add vegetables, salmon, and salmon liquid; heat. Serve over biscuits or toast.

Serves 6

Crunchy Salmon Loaf

1½ cups medium white sauce
3 egg yolks, well beaten
1 (16 oz.) can salmon, drained
    and flaked
2 T. finely chopped onion
1 tsp. paprika

1 (3-oz.) can chow mein
noodles
½ cup almonds (optional)
3 egg whites, stiffly beaten
1½ cups medium white sauce
Sliced hard-cooked eggs
Parsley

Combine 1½ cups medium white sauce and egg yolks in a large mixing bowl. Add salmon, onion, paprika, noodles, and almonds; mix well. Fold in stiffly beaten egg whites. Spoon into a greased 9 x 5 x 3-inch loaf pan. Bake at 375° for 40 to 45 minutes.

Unmold loaf on serving platter. Pour 1½ cups medium white sauce over loaf and garnish with sliced hard-cooked eggs and parsley.

Serves 6-8

CHICKEN DISHES

Chicken-Mac Casserole

1½ cups uncooked elbow
  macaroni
1 cup shredded cheese
1½ cups cooked chicken, cut-
  up
1 (4-oz.) can mushroom stems
  and pieces, drained

¼ cup chopped pimiento
1 can condensed cream of
  chicken soup
1 cup milk
½ tsp. salt
Pepper to taste

Mix all ingredients in an ungreased 1½-quart casserole. Cover
tightly and bake in a 350°-over for 1 hour. (Top with buttered
crumbs and put under broiler for 4 or 5 minutes, if you wish.)

Serves 4-6

Chicken Gumbo

1 cup celery and leaves,
  chopped
1 large onion, chopped
1 T. flour
¼ cup vegetable oil
3 cups chicken broth
1 (16-oz.) can tomatoes
1 green pepper, chopped
1 bay leaf
¼ tsp. thyme

2 cups sliced okra (fresh,
  frozen or canned)
2 T. chopped parsley
Salt to taste
¼ tsp. Tabasco sauce
2 cups coarsely cut, cooked
  chicken
1 (5-oz.) can shrimp, drained
Hot rice

Cook celery, onion and flour in oil 5 minutes, stirring as needed.
Add next 9 ingredients; stir well. Simmer 30 minutes. Stir
occasionally. Add chicken and shrimp, heat through. Serve in soup
bowls with hot rice on top.

Serves 6

Chicken-Corn Bread Casserole

4 cups crumbled corn bread
1/4 cup chopped green pepper
1/4 cup chopped onion
1/4 cup chopped celery

1 1/2 cups coarsely chopped,
   cooked chicken
1 can condensed cream of
   chicken soup
1 1/2 cups chicken broth

Combine corn bread, green pepper, onion and celery; mix well.
Place half of mixture in a 2-quart baking dish. Spread chicken over
corn bread layer.

Combine soup and chicken broth; pour over chicken. Place
remaining corn bread mixture over chicken; press mixture down.
Set aside 20 minutes. Bake at 350° for 45 minutes.

Serves 8-10

Chicken Loaf

4 cups diced chicken (or more)
2 cups fresh bread crumbs
1 cup cooked rice
1 1/2 tsp. salt

3 cups milk or chicken broth
   (or half and half)
1 cup chopped pimiento
4 eggs, well beaten

Mix all the ingredients together, adding eggs last. Pour into a
greased 6-cup baking pan or ring mold. Bake at 325° for 1 hour.
Serve with Mushroom Sauce.

Mushroom Sauce:

1/4 cup butter
1/4 cup flour
2 cups chicken broth
1/4 cup cream
1 (6-oz.) can sliced mushrooms

1 tsp. paprika
1/2 tsp. chopped parsley
1/2 tsp. lemon juice
Salt to taste

Melt the butter in saucepan. Add flour and mix well, and then add
the chicken broth. Cook, stirring constantly until thick and smooth.
Add cream, mushrooms, paprika, parsley, lemon juice, and salt.
Mix and let stand over hot water until ready to serve over chicken.

Serves 8

Chicken a la King

Serve over biscuits, rice, or mashed potatoes.

Blend until smooth:
2 cups prepared chicken soup
4 egg yolks (1 at a time)
2 T. butter or margarine
2 T. flour

Pour into saucepan and cook until sauce thickens. Add to sauce:

2½ to 3 cups coarsely diced chicken, cooked
1 (4-oz.) can mushrooms (or ½ lb. fresh, sautéed)
1 chopped, sautéed green pepper
1 (4-oz.) can sliced pimientos
Heat to serving temperature.

Serves 6

Baked Chicken with Vegetables

1 (4½-lb.) chicken	6 medium carrots
1½ tsp. salt	8 medium new potatoes
1 tsp. paprika	12 to 16 white onions
1 (10½-oz.) can condensed cream of chicken soup	½ cup snipped parsley

Preheat oven to 375°. Sprinkle chicken inside and out with salt; sprinkle outside with paprika. Place in a large, covered Dutch oven or casserole. Mix cream of chicken soup with half a soup-can of water, pour over chicken, then bake, covered, about 1 hour. Meanwhile, pare carrots and potatoes; peel onions; cut carrots, on an angle, into 1-inch chunks; add all 3 vegetables to gravy in Dutch oven; continue baking about one hour, basting chicken once or twice. Now remove cover and continue baking until chicken is golden—about 15 minutes—basting it occasionally. Just before serving, thicken pan juices, if desired; sprinkle with parsley. Serve from Dutch oven, or transfer to heated platter and pass gravy.

Serves 6-8

Chicken Casserole

1 (3-lb.) chicken
1 T. salt
1 (8-oz.) box shell macaroni
½ cup shortening
½ cup chopped onion
3 T. flour
2 tsp. salt

¼ tsp. pepper
½ tsp. basil leaves
½ tsp. oregano leaves
3 cups milk
1 (10-oz.) pkg. frozen green
    peas, thawed
½ cup soft bread crumbs
4 oz. American cheese, diced

Bring 3 quarts water to a boil in large saucepan; add chicken and cook until tender. Remove chicken and reserve broth. Remove chicken from bones and cut into bite-sized pieces. Add 1 tablespoon salt and enough water to reserved broth to make 3 quarts liquid; bring to boil. Gradually add macaroni so that liquid continues to boil. Cook uncovered, stirring occasionally, until tender. Drain in colander, and reserve broth for another dish, if desired.

Meanwhile, in large skillet heat shortening; add onion and sauté until lightly browned. Add flour and remaining seasonings. Gradually add milk and stir over medium heat until sauce boils 2 minutes. Add peas and heat. Combine macaroni, chicken and sauce in 2½-quart casserole. Sprinkle with crumbs and dot with cheese. Bake in 350°-oven 30 minutes.

Serves 6-8

Baked Chicken Hash

2 cups cooked chicken, cut up
1 onion, chopped
1 raw potato, chopped
2 carrots, shredded
Salt and pepper to taste

2 T. chopped parsley
½ tsp. poultry seasoning
1 can condensed cream of
    mushroom or chicken soup

Combine all ingredients and mix well. Put in a casserole, cover and bake in a 350° oven for 45 minutes, then uncover and bake 15 minutes longer.

Serves 4

Cowboy Chicken Casserole

Boil, bone, and cut up large chicken into Dutch oven or casserole dish.

Add:

½ cup chopped onions or onion salt

1 can cream of chicken soup

1 can cream of mushroom soup

1 can Cheddar cheese soup (or sliced Cheddar cheese)

½ can stewed tomatoes with chili peppers

Thoroughly mix all of the above.

Put layer of Taco-flavored Doritos on bottom of dish, then a layer of chicken mixture. Then another layer of Doritos and another of chicken, etc., until completed. Top with cheese if using sliced cheese. Bake at 325° about 45 minutes.

Serves 8

Chicken Tetrazzini

1 stewing chicken (3-4 lbs.) cut up

¼ cup chicken fat

2 T. flour

½ tsp. salt

Pinch cayenne pepper

Chicken broth

½ lb. sliced mushrooms

1 egg yolk, slightly beaten

3 T. light cream

1 cup fine noodles

2 T. grated Parmesan cheese

1 tsp. margarine

Cook chicken. Cut meat from bones in strips. Skim ¼ cup chicken fat from broth. In double boiler, melt 2 tablespoons chicken fat; stir in flour, salt, cayenne, 1 cup chicken broth. Cook, stirring until thickened. Saute mushrooms in 2 tablespoons chicken fat 5 minutes. Into sauce, slowly stir combined egg yolk and cream. Add chicken, mushrooms, heat. Meanwhile, cook noodles in remaining chicken broth (add water if necessary) 10 minutes, or till tender; drain. Arrange noodles in shallow baking dish; pour on chicken mixture, sprinkle with Parmesan cheese; dot with butter. Brown under broiler.

Serves 4-5

Chicken-and-Corn Pie

2 T. butter or margarine
½ lb. small white onions, peeled
½ cup chopped celery
6 T. flour
1 tsp. salt
¼ tsp. pepper
¼ tsp. dried thyme leaves

1 cup chicken broth
1 (12-oz.) can whole-kernel corn
3 cups cooked chicken or turkey, in large pieces
2 hard-cooked eggs, coarsely chopped
Pastry for 1-crust pie
1 egg yolk

Heat butter in large skillet or Dutch oven. Add onions and celery; cook, covered, 10 minutes. Remove from heat. Stir in flour, salt, pepper and thyme until well combined. Gradually stir in chicken broth. Add corn and chicken. Bring to a boil, stirring constantly. Reduce heat; simmer, stirring occasionally, for 10 minutes. Turn into deep 2½-quart casserole or baking dish. Stir in eggs.

Preheat oven to 400°. Make pastry. Roll pastry to fit top of casserole with a ½-inch overhang. Place over chicken mixture; turn edge under; seal to rim of casserole and crimp. Make several slits in top for steam vents. Beat egg yolk with 1 teaspoon water; brush over pastry. Bake 30 minutes, or until crust is deep golden.

Serves 6

Quick Chicken Cacciatore

2 T. salad oil (or olive oil)
1 (2½- to 3-lb.) chicken, cut up
1 onion, peeled, thinly sliced
1 envelope Italian-style spaghetti sauce mix

1 (6-oz.) can tomato paste
1½ cups water
1 tsp. sugar
1 green pepper, cut in strips
Grated Parmesan cheese

In oil, sauté chicken, with onion, until golden. Blend sauce mix, next 4 ingredients; pour over chicken. Simmer for 45 minutes on low heat. Ten minutes before chicken is done add peppers; cook until tender; top with cheese; serve.

Serves 4

Chicken Broccoli Casserole

2 cups chopped broccoli (or asparagas)
1/2 cup minced onions
1 chicken, boiled and boned (ham or turkey)
1 cup shredded Cheddar cheese

White Sauce:

1 small can evaporated milk   2 T. butter
2 T. flour   Salt

Cook until thick.

Place the first ingredients in layers, alternately with the sauce, in a buttered casserole. Sprinkle with paprika. Bake at 325° for 25 minutes.

Serves 4-6

Soupreme Skillet Chicken

2 medium zucchini   1/2 tsp. basil leaves, crushed
2 lbs. chicken parts   1 medium clove garlic, minced
2 T. shortening   1/2 cup drained, chopped,
1 can cream of celery soup   canned tomatoes
1 tsp. paprika

Cut zucchini in half lengthwise; slice diagonally in 1/2-inch pieces. In skillet, brown chicken in shortening; pour off fat. Add soup and seasonings. Cover; cook over low heat 30 minutes. Stir occasionally. Add zucchini and tomatoes. Cook 15 minutes more or until tender.

Serves 4

Quickie Combo

1 (10-oz.) pkg. French-style   1 1/2 cups cooked chicken,
    green beans   cubed
1 can condensed cream of   1/2 tsp. sage
    mushroom soup   chow mein noodles

Cook green beans as directed on label; drain. Combine with soup, chicken and sage, stirring occasionally, until well heated. Serve on chow mein noodles.

Serves 4

Club Chicken Casserole

¼ cup butter or margarine
¼ cup flour
1 cup chicken broth
1 (14¼-oz.) can evaporated
    milk
½ cup water
1½ tsp. salt

3 cups cooked rice
2½ cups diced, cooked chicken
1 (3-oz. can, ¾ cup) broiled
    sliced mushrooms, drained
¼ cup chopped pimiento
⅓ cup chopped green pepper

Melt butter; add flour and blend. Add broth, milk, and water; cook over low heat until thick, stirring constantly. Stir in salt, rice, chicken, and vegetables. Pour into a greased 11½ x 7½ x 1½-inch baking dish. Bake in moderate oven 350° for 30 minutes.

Serves 8-10

Chicken Casserole

Boil a chicken until very tender. Remove from bone and cut into small pieces.

Add:

1 can cream of mushroom
    soup
1 can cream of chicken soup
1 pkg. pure egg noodles
1 small can of pimientos

3 hard-boiled eggs, sliced
2½ cups of the chicken broth
Salt and pepper to taste

Mix all ingredients together and bake until noodles are cooked—about 25 minutes in 375°-oven.

Serves 6

Chicken Combo Casserole

Casserole:

2 cups cooked chicken or turkey or pork or beef, cut in ½-inch.
   cubes
1 cup seasoned bread stuffing cubes
1 (16-oz.) can mixed vegetables; drain, reserving liquid
¼ cup finely chopped onion or 1 T. dried minced onion
2 T. chopped pimiento
1 tsp. salt
¼ tsp. pepper
Reserved ¾ cup liquid (add water if necessary)
¾ to 1 cup mayonnaise or salad dressing

Combine all casserole ingredients. Spread in bottom of ungreased
12 x 8-inch (2-qt.) baking dish. Crumble topping over meat mixture. Bake at 325° for 30-35 minutes until hot. Broil 3-5 minutes
until top is golden and bubbly.

Topping:

¾ cup flour
½ tsp. salt
½ tsp. celery seed

1 cup shredded American
   or Cheddar cheese
¼ cup mayonnaise or salad
   dressing

No need to sift flour; measure by lightly spooning into cup and
leveling off. Combine flour, salt, seed, cheese and mayonnaise;
mix.

Serves 6-8

Zippy Chicken-Cheese Casserole

1 can condensed cream of
   chicken soup
1 (8-oz.) jar cheese spread
½ cup milk
2 cups diced cooked chicken

3 T. chopped green chilies
2 tsp. instant minced onion
4 cups corn chips, coarsely
   crushed

Heat together soup and cheese spread till blended. Gradually add milk; add chicken, chilies and onion. Cook and stir until bubbly. Place ½ of corn chips in 1½-quart casserole. Pour on soup mixture; top with remaining chips. Bake at 350° for 20 minutes. Let stand five minutes.

Serves 4

Peppered Chicken

3 whole chicken breasts
3 small green peppers
1 lb. small onions, peeled
1 (10¾ oz.) can condensed
    chicken broth, undiluted
½ cup water

2 T. cornstarch
1 tsp. salt
6 T. oil
1 clove garlic, crushed
Chow mein noodles or rice
½ cup water

Rinse chicken; skin and bone. Cut chicken into 1-inch chunks. Cut peppers in half; remove seeds and membranes; cut into strips. Cut onions into narrow wedges. Combine chicken broth, water, cornstarch and salt in small bowl. Heat 2 tablespoons oil in kettle or Dutch oven over high heat. Add peppers, onions and garlic. Cook 2 minutes, stirring quickly and constantly with slotted spoon. Remove vegetables to bowl. Heat 2 more tablespoons oil in pan. Add half the chicken. Cook 5 minutes or until lightly browned, stirring occasionally. Remove to bowl. Brown other half of chicken in remaining oil. Return chicken and vegetables to pan. Stir cornstarch mixture; add to chicken. Bring to boiling, stirring constantly. Spoon over chow mein noodles or rice on platter.

Serves 6

Rice with Something Else

Broccoli and Rice

Sauté in 1 or 2 tablespoons margarine:
1/2 cup chopped onion
1/2 cup chopped celery

Cook 1 cup rice in salted water.
Cook 1 pkg. chopped broccoli in salted water. Drain.
Mix rice, broccoli with:
1 can cream chicken soup
1 can cream mushroom soup
1 jar Cheese Whiz (small size)

Put in casserole, sprinkle with paprika.
Bake at 350° for 10 minutes or until bubbly.

Serves 4

Fried Rice with Pork

1 cup uncooked rice
4 T. shortening
3 eggs, beaten
1/2 lb. diced lean pork (or 1 cup diced cooked pork)

1/2 cup chopped green onions
1 1/2 cups thinly sliced celery
3 T. soy sauce

Cook rice according to package directions; drain and set aside.
Heat 1 tablespoon of the shortening in 10-inch skillet; add eggs.
Cook without stirring over low heat until set. Then stir to break up.
Remove eggs and set aside.

Heat remaining 3 tablespoons shortening in same skillet over medium heat. Add pork and fry until well browned. Add onions and celery to pork and fry until onions and celery are tender, about 5 minutes, stirring occasionally. Add soy sauce and reserved rice. Stir over medium heat 2 to 3 minutes; add eggs. Stir until mixture is hot. Serve with additional soy sauce if desired.

Serves 4-6

Curried Rice

2 T. butter or margarine	1 tsp. curry powder
½ cup chopped onion	Juice of 1 lemon
2 cups chicken broth	2 T. parsley flakes
1 tsp. salt	1 cup regular uncooked rice
⅛ tsp. pepper	Dash paprika (optional)

Melt butter in a 2-quart sauce pan; add onion, cooking slowly until tender. Combine chicken broth, salt, pepper, curry, lemon juice, and parsley flakes.

Spoon curried sauce over servings of rice (cooked according to package directions).

Serves 4

Chicken and Rice

Cook: 1 small box brown rice

Add: 1 can beef bouillon soup
¼ cup onions, chopped
¼ cup chopped celery
1 small can mushrooms

Pour into baking dish, top with chicken and bake 45 minutes to 1 hour. Serve while hot.

Serves 4-6

Chicken and Rice II

1½ cups uncooked rice (25 min. cooking rice)	1 stick melted butter
	1 pkg. dry onion soup mix
1 or 2 raw chickens, cut up	3 cups water
	Salt and pepper

Place uncooked rice in bottom of large Pyrex dish. Arrange chicken on top of rice. Salt and pepper chicken. Pour melted butter over chicken mix and sprinkle onion soup mix over it. Add water. Cover. Bake in 350°-oven for 2 hours.

Serves 6-8

Baked Rice Dish

½ cup uncooked rice
1 cup beef bouillon soup
½ cup water
½ stick margarine

½ tsp. salt
⅛ tsp. garlic salt
Pepper to taste

Grease casserole dish and fill with mixed ingredients. Bake 1 hour and 15 minutes at 325°, covered.

Serves 4

Green Rice

2 cups cooked rice
1 cup chopped green pepper
1 cup chopped parsley

1 cup grated cheese
½ cup salad oil
1 or 2 cloves garlic, minced

Mix all ingredients together. Place in greased baking dish. Pour enough milk on until you see it at top layer. Bake at 350° until milk is absorbed (about 45 minutes).

Serves 4-6

Spam 'n Rice

¼ cup chopped onions
¼ cup diced green pepper
1 small clove garlic, minced
2 T. oil
2 cups (16-oz. can) tomatoes
(cut in small pieces)

1 cup uncooked white rice
1 cup frozen green peas
1 cup hot water
½ tsp. salt
1 tsp. oregano
Dash black pepper
1 (11-oz.) can Spam

In deep skillet, over low heat, cook onions and green pepper in oil and garlic until tender. Add remaining ingredients except Spam. Cut Spam into six even slices and place in center of skillet. Bring to boil. Cover, cook over low heat until rice is tender and has absorbed the extra liquid. As an added touch, heat ½ cup tomato sauce and pour over Spam just before serving.

Serves 6

Fried Rice

2 cups cooked rice
10 slices bacon
1 cup onions

6 eggs
1/3 can bean sprouts

Cook rice to separated stage. In a skillet, fry bacon, then remove; brown onions and take out of skillet. Pour out one half of grease and scramble eggs. Mix rice, crumbled bacon and onions in scrambled eggs; add bean sprouts. Season to taste with soy sauce. Ham can be substituted for bacon.

Serves 6

Cheese and Rice Casserole

3 cups cooked, regular rice
2 cups shredded Cheddar
    cheese
2 T. finely chopped green
    pepper

2 eggs, beaten
1 1/4 cups milk
1 tsp. salt
Dash of cayenne pepper
1/2 cup buttered bread crumbs

Alternate layers of rice, cheese, and green pepper in a greased 1 1/2-quart casserole dish.
    Combine eggs, milk, salt, and cayenne; pour over casserole. Sprinkle bread crumbs over top. Bake at 350° about 45 minutes or until set.

Serves 6

Spanish Rice

2 cloves garlic, minced
1/4 cup oil
1 cup uncooked rice
1 lb. hamburger

2 T. chili powder
1 can tomatoes
Salt and pepper to taste

Brown rice in cooking oil. When rice begins to brown add garlic, then hamburger, chili powder, salt and pepper. When browned add tomatoes and water to cover. Cook in covered skillet until rice is tender.

Serves 6

Italian Rice Casserole

1 cup chopped onion
½ cup chopped green pepper
½ cup chopped celery
1 T. salad oil
1 lb. ground beef
1 (8-oz.) can tomatoes
1 (6-oz.) can tomato paste
1 (4-oz.) can mushroom pieces,
    drained

2 T. chopped parsley
1 tsp. salt
½ tsp. thyme
½ tsp. pepper
¼ tsp. marjoram
1 cup uncooked rice
½ cup shredded Cheddar
    cheese

Sauté onion, green pepper, and celery in oil until almost transparent; add beef and cook until brown. Stir in tomatoes, tomato paste, mushrooms, parsley, and seasonings. Simmer 1 hour over low heat.

Cook rice according to package directions. Combine rice and meat mixture in a shallow baking dish. Sprinkle with cheese. Bake at 400° for 15 minutes.

Serves 6

Mexican Rice

2 T. oil
1 cup uncooked rice
1 cup tomatoes
1 small onion, minced

½ green pepper, chopped
2 tsp. salt
2 tsp. chili powder

Brown rice in fat, add onion, green pepper, salt, chili powder, tomatoes. Mix well; add enough water to cover. Cover with lid and allow to simmer till rice is tender (about 30 minutes). Do not stir after cooking starts. Remove lid to allow mixture to dry out.

Serves 4

Spaghetti, Macaroni, Noodle Dishes

French Spaghetti

Serve with French bread toasted with garlic butter.

2 (8-oz.) boxes of thin, long spaghetti
1 large round steak (1 or 1½ lbs.)
½ lb. grated Cheddar cheese
1 can tomatoes
1 can small green peas
Garlic powder suited to the family's taste for garlic
¼ lb. margarine (1 stick)
Salt, pepper, paprika (suit to taste)

Cook spaghetti according to directions on package. Drain and rinse. Cube steak and brown lightly in margarine. Add garlic powder, salt, and pepper to meat. Add remainder of ingredients, except cheese, to spaghetti. Cook over low flame until well seasoned (20 to 30 minutes). Add cheese and allow to melt.

Serves 8

Mexitalian Spaghetti

Serve with tossed salad and French bread with garlic butter.

1 lb. hamburger
1½ cups chopped onion
¾ cup chopped green pepper
3 cloves garlic, chopped
3 (8-oz. cans) (3 cups)
    seasoned tomato sauce
1 (6-oz. can) (⅔ cup) tomato
    paste
⅓ cup water
2 tsp. Worcestershire sauce
1½ tsp. salt
Dash pepper
1 (16-oz.) package spaghetti,
    cooked

Brown meat; drain off excess fat. Add onion, pepper, and garlic; cook 1 minute. Add tomato sauce, tomato paste, water, Worcestershire sauce, salt, pepper. Cover and simmer 2 hours. Serve sauce over hot spaghetti.

Serves 8-10

Spaghetti Parmesan

1 can mushrooms
1 stick butter or margarine
4 or 5 slices crisp bacon, crumbled

1 (8-oz.) box spaghetti
1 carton sour cream
1 small can Parmesan cheese

Prepare spaghetti, rinse in cold water and set aside. Saute mushrooms in ½ stick butter. Add bacon and simmer about 2 or 3 minutes. Combine sour cream, spaghetti and Parmesan cheese, and add to mushroom mixture and heat thoroughly.

Serves 4-6

Hurry-Spaghetti Supper

1 lb. ground beef
1 onion, chopped
1 clove garlic, minced
2 (6-oz.) cans tomato paste
3 cups water

1 tsp. salt
1 tsp. sugar
½ tsp. oregano
½ tsp. basil
¼ tsp. pepper

Lightly brown beef, onion and garlic; drain fat. Stir in remaining ingredients. Simmer, uncovered, one hour. Serve over hot spaghetti.

Serves 4

Parslied Spaghetti

1 T. salt
3 qts. boiling water
8 oz. spaghetti

2 cloves garlic, minced
½ cup butter or margarine, melted
½ cup finely chopped parsley

Add 1 tablespoon salt to rapidly boiling water. Gradually add spaghetti so that water continues to boil. Cook uncovered, stirring occasionally, until tender. Drain in colander.

Brown garlic in butter. Add, with parsley, to spaghetti. Toss.

Serves 4

Spaghetti with Meatballs

1 lb. ground beef
1 tsp. salt
$1/8$ tsp. pepper
2 T. grated onion
2 T. oil
8-10 oz. pkg. spaghetti, cooked
1 can tomato soup

$1/2$ soup can, water
2 (8 oz.) cans tomato sauce
$1/2$ tsp. salt
$1/4$ tsp. celery salt
1 tsp. oregano
1 T. Worcestershire sauce
4 slices bacon

Mix first four ingredients well. Shape into 12 balls. Brown well in hot oil. Now heat in saucepan the tomato soup, water, sauce, and seasonings. Drain fat from hamburger. Add the heated sauce to the meatballs in skillet and simmer for 30 minutes. Fry the bacon until crisp. Drain off fat. Crumble the bacon. Serve the cooked spaghetti on a platter, topped with the sauce and meatballs. Sprinkle bacon on top.

Serves 4-6

Spaghetti with Meat Sauce

1 (12 or 16-oz.) pkg. spaghetti
  (prepare according to pkg.)
1 medium onion, chopped
2 T. olive oil
1 lb. ground beef
1 clove garlic, minced
$1/2$ cup chopped parsley
$1/2$ tsp. oregano

1 small can mushrooms
1 tsp. salt
$1/4$ tsp. pepper
1 tsp. marjoram
1 cup water
1 (20-oz.) can tomatoes
1 (6-oz.) can tomato paste
Parmesan cheese

Sauté chopped onion in olive oil for five minutes. Remove onion; add ground beef and fry until brown, stirring frequently. Return onion to skillet. Add garlic, parsley, oregano, tomatoes and tomato paste. Add mushrooms, remaining seasonings and water. Simmer slowly. Spoon sauce over spaghetti. Top with Parmesan cheese.

Serves 4-6

Ham and Spaghetti Casserole

3 T. butter or margarine
¼ cup all-purpose flour
½ tsp. salt
½ white pepper
3 cups milk
1 cup shredded American
    cheese

1 cup cubed cooked ham
1 (7-oz.) package spaghetti,
    cooked and drained
Sliced hard-cooked eggs
    (optional)

Melt butter in large saucepan; blend in flour, salt and white pepper. Gradually add milk, stirring until thickened. Remove from heat and blend in cheese; add ham and cooked spaghetti. Stir in eggs slowly.

Serves 4-6

Spaghetti Sauce I

3½ lbs. ground beef
¾ cup oil
2 (16-oz.) cans tomatoes
4 green peppers, finely
    chopped
6 large onions, finely chopped
Finely chopped garlic, to taste

1 bunch celery, finely chopped
Chili powder, to taste
2 (6-oz.) cans tomato paste
2 (4-oz.) cans sliced
    mushrooms

Brown meat in cooking oil and add other ingredients. *Simmer over low heat for 6 hours.

    Note—since this is a large quantity of sauce, you will need to cook it in one very large pan or divide it and cook in two large skillets. Serve immediately with prepared spaghetti or place in freezer containers and freeze.

Makes 5 quarts sauce

*The secret of a good spaghetti sauce is to simmer it long enough to make the flavors blend well together. You may not be able to simmer it as long as is indicated; but the longer the better. A crock-pot is ideal for this.

Spaghetti Sauce II

6 cans tomatoes, sieved
3 small cans tomato paste
2 small cans tomato sauce
1 can tomato juice

1 medium onion (cut small)
3 cloves garlic, minced
2-3 T. Romano cheese

Put tomatoes and juice in large pot with onion and garlic; bring to boil. Add tomato sauce and tomato paste (bring to boil). Let boil few minutes. Simmer 1½ to 2 hours.

Spaghetti Sauce III

¼ cup celery
1 small green pepper, chopped
1 minced onion—sauted
1 small can mushrooms
1 can tomatoes

1 can tomato paste
1 clove garlic, minced
Rosemary to taste
2 bay leaves

Simmer 1½ to 2 hours. Add 1 or 1½ pounds freshly ground meat. Cook slowly until completely done.

Spaghetti with Tuna Sauce

1 (10½ oz.) can beef
    consomme
1¼ cups water
⅓ cup flour
2 T. horseradish
2 tsp. Worcestershire sauce
2 T. butter or margarine

2 (7-oz.) cans chunk-style
    tuna, drained
¼ cup chopped parsley
1 T. salt
3 qts. boiling water
8 oz. spaghetti

Heat beef consommé to boiling point. Combine 1¼ cups water and flour; mix well. Add to consommé and cook over low heat until thickened, stirring constantly. Add horseradish, Worcestershire, butter, tuna and parsley; cook over low heat 10 minutes, stirring constantly.

Meanwhile, add 1 tablespoon salt to rapidly boiling water. Gradually add spaghetti so that water continues to boil. Cook uncovered, stirring ocasionally, until tender. Drain in colander. Serve tuna sauce over hot spaghetti.

Serves 4

Firecracker Macaroni and Cheese

2 T. salt
4 to 6 qts. boiling water
4 cups elbow macaroni (16 oz.)
1 medium onion, chopped
½ cup chopped celery
⅓ cup butter or margarine
⅓ cup flour

3 cups milk
1 cup heavy cream
1 tsp. salt
1 tsp. crushed red pepper
    (or 1½ tsp. chili powder)
1 tsp. Worcestershire sauce
4 cups grated, sharp Cheddar
    cheese (about 1 lb.)

Add 2 tablespoons salt to rapidly boiling water. Gradually add macaroni so that water continues to boil. Cook uncovered, stirring occasionally, until tender. Drain in colander.

Meanwhile, in medium saucepan saute onion and celery in butter until crisp-tender; stir in flour. Gradually add milk and cream; cook, stirring constantly, until sauce boils 1 minute. Remove from heat. Add remaining seasonings and 3 cups of the cheese. Stir until cheese melts. Combine macaroni and sauce; turn into 3-quart baking dish. Sprinkle remaining cheese on top. Bake uncovered in 375°-oven 15 to 20 minutes, until bubbly.

Serves 8

Baked Macaroni and Cheese

1 cup uncooked macaroni
3 eggs, beaten
3 cups milk
½ lb. Cheddar cheese, cut in
    cubes

Salt and pepper to taste
2 T. margarine
Paprika (optional)

Cook macaroni according to package directions; drain. Combine eggs and milk in a large bowl; add macaroni, cheese, salt and pepper. Spoon mixture into a 2-quart casserole dish; dot with margarine, and sprinkle with paprika, if desired. Bake at 325° for 40 to 60 minutes, or until set.

Serves 6

Pepper Noodles

1 (7¼-oz.) pkg. macaroni and
  cheese dinner
1 lb. lean ground beef
½ cup chopped green pepper
¼ cup chopped onion
1 (8-oz.) can tomato sauce

Prepare macaroni and cheese dinner according to package directions. Meanwhile, in skillet brown ground beef with green pepper and onion; pour off excess fat. Combine beef, macaroni dinner and tomato sauce; simmer over very low heat until heated through; stir occasionally.

Serves 4-6

Noodles, Salmon and Peas

1 (5-oz.) package wide noodles
¼ cup flour
1 tsp. salt
¼ tsp. pepper
½ tsp. dry mustard
¼ cup melted butter or
  margarine
1 (16-oz.) can salmon
Light cream
1 small onion, grated
2 small cans pimientos, diced
2 T. minced parsley
2 eggs, beaten
2 (16-oz.) cans green peas
2 T. butter or margarine

Cook noodles according to package directions; rinse and drain.
  Blend flour and seasonings into ¼ cup melted butter. Drain liquid from salmon and add enough light cream to make 2 cups. Add to flour mixture and cook until thickened, stirring constantly. Remove from heat.
  Add noodles, onion, pimiento, parsley and eggs to sauce. Gently stir in salmon, which has been broken into bite-size chunks. Spoon into a buttered ring mold. Bake at 350° for about 45 minutes or until firm. Heat peas and add 2 tablespoons butter. Loosen salmon ring around edges and turn out on a large platter; fill center with peas.

Serves 6-8

Noodles and Ham Casserole

1 T. salt
3 qts. boiling water
8 oz. wide egg noodles
1 cup chicken bouillon or
    stock
2 cups diced cooked ham

1 (3-oz.) can sliced mushrooms
¼ cup nonfat dry-milk solids
1 tsp. dry mustard
1 tsp. onion salt
1 tsp. butter or margarine

Add 1 tablespoon salt to rapidly boiling water. Gradually add noodles so that water continues to boil. Cook uncovered, stirring occasionally, until tender. Drain in colander. Meanwhile, mix together bouillon, ham, undrained mushrooms, dry-milk solids, mustard and onion salt. Add noodles; mix well. Turn noodle mixture into buttered 2-quart casserole and bake in 350°-oven 1 hour.

Serves 4

Macaroni Cheese Deluxe

Sour cream makes this saucy casserole extra good and company-elegant.

1 7-oz. pkg. (1¾ cup) elbow
    macaroni
2 cups small curd, cream-style
    cottage cheese
1 cup dairy sour cream
1 slightly beaten egg

¾ tsp. salt
Dash pepper
8 oz. sharp process American
    cheese, shredded (2 cups)
Paprika

Cook macaroni according to package directions; drain well. Combine cottage cheese, sour cream, egg, salt, and pepper. Add cheese, mixing well; stir in cooked macaroni. Turn into greased 9 x 9 x 2 in. baking dish. Sprinkle with paprika. Bake in 350° oven for 45 minutes.

Serves 6-8

Macaroni and Cheese

1 T. salt
3 qts. boiling water
2 cups elbow macaroni (8 oz.)
2 tsp. butter or margarine
1 T. flour
3 T. nonfat dry-milk solids

1 cup water
1 cup creamed cottage cheese
1 tsp. garlic salt
1 tsp. caraway seeds
$1/8$ tsp. pepper
$1/2$ cup grated American cheese

Add 1 tablespoon salt to 3 quarts rapidly boiling water. Gradually add macaroni so that water continues to boil. Cook uncovered, stirring occasionally, until tender. Drain in colander.

Melt 2 teaspoons butter, blend in flour and milk solids. Gradually add 1 cup water and cook over low heat, stirring constantly, until thickened. Stir in cottage cheese, seasonings and macaroni. Turn macaroni mixture into greased casserole and top with American cheese. Bake in 350°-oven 1 hour.

Serves 6

Macaroni Chicken Salad

1 T. salt
3 qts. boiling water
2 cups elbow macaroni (8 oz.)
2 cups diced, cooked chicken
1 cup diced celery
2 sweet gherkins, chopped
2 T. chopped onion

1 small can pimiento, chopped
$1/3$ cup mayonnaise
Juice of 1 medium lemon
$1/8$ tsp. dry mustard
Dash Tabasco sauce
1 medium tomato, cut in 8
   wedges

Add 1 tablespoon salt to rapidly boiling water. Gradually add macaroni so that water continues to boil. Cook uncovered, stirring occasionally, until tender. Drain in colander. Rinse with cold water; drain again.

Combine and toss macaroni, chicken, celery, gherkins, onion, pimiento, mayonnaise, lemon juice, and seasonings. Chill. Garnish with tomato wedges.

Serves 6-8

Creamy Meatballs and Noodles

1 lb. lean ground beef
½ cup finely chopped onion
¼ cup cracker crumbs
1 egg
¼ cup milk
1 tsp. salt
½ tsp. nutmeg

1 T. oil
2 beef bouillon cubes, dissolved
  in 1 cup water
1 (8-oz.) can tomato sauce
1 T. cornstarch
1 cup sour cream
Hot cooked noodles

Mix first 7 ingredients; shape into balls. Brown in oil in skillet. Remove fat. Add bouillon. Mix tomato sauce and cornstarch; add to skillet. Simmer uncovered 25 minutes; stir occasionally. *Add a little sauce from skillet to sour cream, stir, add cream to skillet; stir gently. Serve over noodles.

Serves 4

*This must be done to prevent curdling.

Bacon-Noodle Skillet

1 (1-lb.) package bacon
⅓ cup chopped green pepper
⅓ cup chopped onion
1 tsp. salt
½ tsp. marjoram
½ tsp. thyme

⅛ tsp. pepper
1 (29-oz.) can tomatoes
1 (6-oz.) package wide noodles,
  uncooked
1 cup shredded process
  American cheese

Cook bacon to desired crispness; drain and crumble. Pour off all drippings except 2 tablespoons; add green pepper, onion, and seasonings to drippings and cook 5 minutes. Add tomatoes and bring to a boil. Add noodles; cover and simmer 20 minutes.

Stir in half of crumbled bacon. Top with cheese and remaining bacon; cover and heat 5 minutes.

Serves 6

Confetti Beef and Macaroni

1 lb. ground beef
1 cup chopped onion
1 cup sliced celery
1 (10-oz.) pkg. frozen mixed
    vegetables
2 (8-oz.) cans tomato sauce
    with cheese

$^{1}/_{2}$ cup water
1 tsp. Worcestershire sauce
$^{1}/_{2}$ tsp. salt
$^{1}/_{8}$ tsp. pepper
2 cups cooked macaroni

Brown beef in skillet; add onion, celery, and mixed vegetables.
Cook until onion is tender. Remove fat. Add tomato sauce, water,
Worcestershire sauce, salt and pepper. Stir in macaroni. Cover
and simmer 15 minutes.

Serves 6

Chuck Wagon Macaroni

1 7- or 8-oz. pkg. (2 cups)
    macaroni
$^{1}/_{2}$ cup butter or margarine
$^{1}/_{4}$ cup chili sauce

1 tsp. Worcestershire sauce
$^{1}/_{2}$ lb. sharp process American
    cheese, shredded (2 cups)
Paprika (optional)

In large saucepan, cook macaroni according to package
directions; drain well. Return cooked macaroni to saucepan; add
butter or margarine, chili sauce, and Worcestershire sauce; heat till
butter is melted. Add shredded cheese; stir till melted and well
mixed. Sprinkle with paprika if desired. Serve immediately.

Serves 4-6

SANDWICHES

Burger Mushroom Bake

1 can mushroom soup
1½ lbs. ground beef
½ cup fine, dry bread crumbs

1 egg, slightly beaten
¼ cup finely chopped onion
⅓ cup water

Combine ¼ cup soup with remaining ingredients except water; mix thoroughly. Shape into 6 patties; place in shallow baking dish (12 x 8 x 2-in.). Bake at 350° for 30 minutes. Spoon off fat. Combine remaining soup and water; pour over meat. Bake 10 minutes longer. Serve on hamburger buns.

Serves 6

Burger Baste

Helps dress-up thrifty burgers, franks, chicken.

1 (6-oz.) can tomato paste
1 cup water
½ cup bottled steak sauce
⅓ cup lemon juice

⅓ cup brown sugar
¼ cup oil
¼ cup minced onions

Simmer 15 minutes.

Makes 2½ cups barbecue sauce

Chili Cheese Franks

2 (16-oz.) cans chili with beans
1 can condensed Cheddar
  cheese soup
2 T. instant minced onion

1 lb. (8-10) frankfurters
8-10 frankfurter buns, split and
  toasted
Corn chips, coarsely crushed

In large saucepan combine chili, cheese soup, and onion. Add frankfurters; heat to boiling. Simmer mixture about 5 minutes to blend flavors. To serve, place a frankfurter on each toasted frankfurter bun; top each with chili-cheese sauce and sprinkle with crushed corn chips.

Serves 8-10

Hot Western Sandwiches

8 frankfurter rolls
Butter or margarine
1/3 cup each, finely chopped
    green onion and green
    pepper
3/4 cup minced ham

6 eggs, slightly beaten
3/4 cup milk
1/2 tsp. salt
Freshly ground black pepper
Grated Parmesan cheese

Open rolls, spread with butter and place, buttered side up, on baking sheet. In skillet, melt 1 tablespoon butter. Add green onion, pepper and ham and saute, stirring, a few minutes. Transfer to mixing bowl. Cool slightly, then stir in eggs, milk and seasonings. In small buttered heated skillet, cook 8 individual omelets, using about 1/2 cup egg mixture for each. Cook only until still slightly creamy. Roll up and place one on bottom part of each roll. Sprinkle with cheese and, just before serving, toast under broiler 2 minutes. Close sandwiches and serve at once.

Serves 8

Chili Cheese Burgers

1 envelope chili mix
1 (16-oz.) can tomatoes
1 1/2 lbs. ground beef

3/4 cup shredded Cheddar or
    American cheese
1 (16-oz.) can kidney beans,
    drained
6-8 hamburger rolls

Stir together contents of chili mix envelope and tomatoes in sauce pan; add 1/2 cup of this mixture to the ground beef and cheese in a mixing bowl. Shape 6 to 8 patties. Add beans to remaining chili mixture in sauce pan; simmer 10 minutes, stirring occasionally. Grill patties over hot coals until done, 10 to 15 minutes. Serve each patty on a roll, topped with a generous spoonful of chili mixture.

Serves 6-8

Open-Faced Broiled Sandwiches

4 slices of bread   4 tsp. butter
4 slices of cheese   8 slices of bacon
4 slices of tomatoes

Cook bacon. Spread butter on bread then place tomato slices, bacon, and cheese. Broil until cheese melts.

Serves 4

Salmon Burgers

1 (16-oz.) can salmon   1 tsp. prepared mustard
½ cup chopped onion   ½ tsp. salt
¼ cup melted margarine ½ cup dry bread crumbs
⅓ cup dry bread crumbs Shortening for frying
2 eggs, beaten   6 buttered hamburger rolls

Drain liquid from salmon; reserve liquid. Break salmon into small pieces.

Saute onion in margarine until tender. Mix onion, ⅓ cup bread crumbs, eggs, mustard, salt, salmon, and salmon liquid. Make 6 patties. Coat patties with ½ cup bread crumbs and fry in hot shortening for 3 to 4 minutes on each side or until brown. Drain on paper towels. Serve on warm hamburger rolls.

Serves 6

MEAT,
POULTRY,
AND FISH

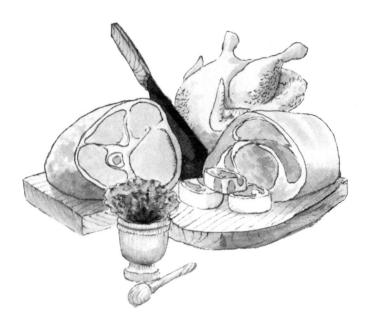

CHICKEN

Chicken Continental

3-4 lbs. chicken pieces (thighs, legs, breasts)
1/3 cup seasoned flour
1/4 cup shortening
1 can cream of chicken soup
2 1/2 T. grated onion
1 tsp. salt
1 T. chopped parsley
1/8 tsp. thyme
1/2 tsp. celery flakes
1 1/3 cup water
1 1/3 cup minute rice
1/2 tsp. paprika

Roll chicken in flour, sauté in shortening until golden brown. Mix soup, onion, seasonings in saucepan. Gradually stir in water and bring to boil, stirring constantly. Pour rice into shallow 2-quart casserole. Stir in all but 1/3 soup mixture. Top with chicken and pour on remaining soup mixture. Cover. Bake 1 hour at 375°. Sprinkle with paprika.

Serves 4-6

Golden-Glazed Chicken

1 (3 1/2 lb.) broiler-fryer cut into serving pieces
1/3 cup flour
1 tsp. salt
1/2 tsp. poultry seasoning
1/4 tsp. paprika
1/4 cup shortening
1/4 cup orange gelatin powder
3/4 cup pineapple juice
1 cup pineapple slices
2 oranges, cut in wedges, or pineapples slices, for garnish
Parsley sprigs

Wash chicken, pat dry. Combine flour, poultry seasoning, salt and paprika in paper bag. Place chicken in bag, shake. Heat shortening in pan; brown chicken lightly. Place chicken in casserole; bake 30 minutes. Dissolve gelatin in boiling pineapple juice. Pour over chicken; arrange pineapple slices around edge. Bake about 40 minutes until golden and tender, basting with pineapple juice and gelatin mixture. Arrange on platter. Garnish with either orange wedges or pineapple slices and parsley.

Serves 4-6

Oven-Fried Hawaiian Chicken

Serve with fluffy rice.

2 fryers (2½ to 3 lbs. each)
   cut in pieces
½ cup soy sauce
2 T. grated onion
1 tsp. ground ginger
½ cup cornstarch

½ cup margarine
4 T. lemon juice
1 (20-oz.) can pineapple
   chunks, undrained
1 (20-oz.) can pineapple juice

Place the chicken pieces in a large bowl. Combine soy sauce, onion and ginger and pour over chicken. Let stand for 1 hour, turning the chicken to coat all sides. Drain chicken and coat with cornstarch. Reserve the marinade. Place the margarine in a large, shallow baking pan, set in a 375°-oven until melted. Add chicken (use two pans if you cannot get all the pieces in one pan in a single layer). Bake for 30 minutes, skin down, then turn. Combine pineapple with the liquid, lemon juice and the marinade sauce; pour over the chicken and bake 20 minutes longer or until tender.

Serves 8

Swellickins

8 chicken wings
1½ tsp. instant meat marinade
⅓ cup cold water
¾ cup biscuit mix
½ cup shortening

Remove wing tips, separate wings at joint. Combine marinade and water in plastic bag; drop in chicken and seal. Marinate 15 minutes.

While chicken is marinating, preheat skillet to moderate heat. Add shortening. Dip chicken in biscuit mix, coating well. Place chicken in hot shortening in skillet; cook until nicely browned on both sides. Reduce temperature, and cook 20 minutes, or until fork-tender.

Makes 16 hors d'oeuvres

Chicken Wing Ding

2 lbs. chicken wings
Salt
3½ T. (½ envelope) onion
 soup mix

1 cup dairy sour cream
1 cup flour
2 cups shortening

Tuck under chicken wing tips and sprinkle wings lightly with salt. Blend onion soup mix and sour cream. Using a pastry brush, spread sour cream mixture on chicken wings, covering completely. (If mixture seems too thick, thin with a little milk.) Roll chicken in flour; let stand 10 minutes, then roll again in flour. In a large skillet, heat shortening. Cook chicken, half at a time, in hot shortening until browned on all sides. Return all browned chicken to pan; cover and reduce heat. Cook 15 minutes, turning wings occasionally. Drain on paper towels. Serve hot or cold.

Serves 4

Foil-Baked Chicken

With this chicken barbecue you'll have no grill or broiler pan to clean.

½ cup water
⅓ cup catsup
⅓ cup vinegar
¼ cup brown sugar
4 T. butter or margarine,
 melted
2 T. Worcestershire sauce

2 T. lemon juice
2 tsp. salt
2 tsp. paprika
2 tsp. chili powder
2 tsp. dry mustard
2 (2½ to 3 lb.) broiler-fryers, cut
 up

In bowl, blend together all ingredients except chicken. Divide chicken in 4 to 6 serving-size portions. Dip chicken pieces in sauce, placing each serving on separate piece of heavy foil. Pour about 1 tablespoon sauce over each portion of chicken; seal foil securely. Bake in 400° oven for 45 minutes. Open foil packets; brush with remaining sauce. Bake 15 minutes longer.

Serves 4-6

Easy Chicken Bake

Cut up fryer-chicken; salt and pepper; dip in butter (1 stick melted) and place in shallow baking pan. Place under broiler and brown both sides. Mix 1 chicken bouillon cube in a cup of hot water and pour over browned chicken. Cover pan with foil and let cook about 30 minutes at 350°. Good served with Chicken Rice-A-Roni. Juice from chicken makes good gravy.

Serves 4

Chicken Crunch

1 can cream of mushroom soup
¾ cup water
1 T. finely chopped onion
2 lbs. chicken parts
1 cup finely crushed, packaged herb-seasoned stuffing
2 T. melted butter or margarine

Mix ⅓ cup soup, ¼ cup water, and onion. Dip chicken in soup mixture; roll in stuffing. Place in shallow baking dish (12 x 8 x 2"); drizzle with butter. Bake at 400° for one hour. Combine remaining soup, water. Heat; stir. Serve over chicken.

Serves 4

Barbecued Chicken

Mix together and simmer:

1 medium, chopped onion	1 cup catsup
2 T. oil	1 cup water
2 T. vinegar	3 T. Worcestershire sauce
2 T. brown sugar	½ T. prepared mustard
Dash red pepper and celery salt	Salt and pepper

Put the cut-up pieces of one frying chicken into the sauce and simmer for about 30 minutes. Then remove the chicken and brown for about 15 minutes or until done on a charcoal grill or broiler. Dip the pieces of chicken into the sauce from time to time. Add more salt, while broiling.

Serves 4

Oven-Fried Parmesan Chicken

¾ cup butter or margarine
3 broiler-fryer chickens cut into
   serving pieces
3 tsp. salt
1½ tsp. monosodium
   glutamate (Accent)
¼ tsp. pepper

1½ cups flour
½ cup grated Parmesan cheese
½ tsp. paprika
1½ tsp. oregano
1 cup buttermilk

Line two 15 x 10 x 1-inch shallow pans with foil. Divide butter between pans. Put in 425°-oven until butter melts (about 5 minutes). Sprinkle chicken pieces with half the salt, accent and pepper. Turn chicken, sprinkle with remaining half of seasonings. Combine flour, cheese, paprika and oregano. Dip chicken in buttermilk, then in flour mixture. Place skin down in melted butter. Bake at 425° for 30 minutes. Turn chicken, reverse pans on shelves, bake 20 minutes longer.

Serves 12.

Chicken with Spiced Peach Sauce

Combine in saucepan and cook over very low heat, 1 cup orange juice, 1½ cups sliced, canned or frozen peaches, 2 tablespoons brown sugar, 2 tablespoons vinegar, 1 teaspoon nutmeg, 1 teaspoon basil, 1 clove garlic, minced.

   Cut into serving pieces, two 2½ pound broiler-fryers. Coat chicken pieces with ½ cup flour seasoned with salt and pepper. In 12-inch skillet, fry chicken in hot oil, over medium heat, until browned. Pour sauce over chicken. Cover and simmer over low heat 20 to 30 minutes or until chicken is tender.

Serves 6

Chicken Scallopini

8 broiler-fryer chicken thighs, boned
1 tsp. salt
2 T. butter or margarine
1 T. lemon juice
2 T. chopped parsley
1 T. chopped chives or green onions
1/4 tsp. marjoram

Place chicken between 2 pieces of aluminum foil; pound with side of cleaver or rolling pin to flatten. Sprinkle with salt. Melt butter over medium heat in large skillet. Add chicken, skin side down; saute about 10 minutes or until lightly browned. Turn chicken, and sprinkle with lemon juice and herbs; continue cooking until tender. Serve hot.

Serves 4

MEATBALLS

Meatballs

1 lb. ground meat
2 T. green pepper, chopped
2 T. onion, chopped
1 tsp. chili powder
1/2 tsp. dry mustard
1 egg
1/2 cup milk
1/4 cup cornmeal

Mix above ingredients. Form balls, roll in 1/2 cup flour, and brown in shortening. Sprinkle remaining flour over meatballs. Add one medium can tomato juice and simmer for 45 minutes to 1 hour.

Serves 4

Sweet and Sour Meatballs

Serve with hot buttered noodles.

1 lb. ground beef
1 egg, beaten
1/4 cup dry bread crumbs
1/2 tsp. salt
1/4 tsp. ginger
1/4 cup flour
3 T. oil
1 (20-oz.) can pineapple
   chunks
2 T. brown sugar
3/4 tsp. cornstarch
1/4 cup vinegar
1 T. soy sauce
2 green peppers, seeded and
   cut into strips

Mix ground beef with egg, crumbs and seasonings; form into 16 balls. Dredge meatballs in flour; brown in oil in large frying pan. Remove meatballs from pan. Drain pineapple, reserving liquid; add water to syrup to make 1 cup. Stir into drippings in pan. Mix brown sugar with cornstarch, vinegar and soy sauce. Add to syrup mixture. Cook, stirring constantly, until sauce is thickened and clear. Arrange meatballs, pineapple chunks and pepper strips separately in pan; stir each gently to coat with sauce. Cover; simmer for 10 minutes or until green pepper is tender, but still crisp.

Serves 4

Chili Meatballs

1 lb. hamburger
2 T. green pepper, chopped
2 T. onion, chopped
1 tsp. chili powder

½ tsp. dry mustard
1 egg
½ cup milk
¼ cup cornmeal

Mix above ingredients. Form balls, roll in ½ cup flour, and brown in shortening. Sprinkle remaining flour over meat balls. Add one medium can tomato juice and simmer for 45 minutes to 1 hour.

Serves 4

Sauce-Pot Meatballs

1 pkg. dry onion soup mix
1¼ cups water
2 (8-oz.) cans tomato sauce
1 lb. hamburger

½ tsp. garlic salt
½ tsp. thyme
¼ tsp. pepper
1 T. chopped parsley

In deep, heavy saucepan, bring to a boil quickly the onion soup mix, water and 1½ cans tomato sauce. Simmer, covered, for 10 minutes. Mix ground beef, seasonings, parsley and remaining tomato sauce. Shape into 16 meatballs and place them in sauce. Simmer gently, uncovered, for 25 minutes, turning occasionally. Serve over hot noodles, spaghetti, or rice, with grated Parmesan cheese, toast with garlic butter and salad.

Sauce and meatballs freeze well; thaw, heat slowly and pour over noodles, spaghetti, or rice.

Serves 4

Spicy Meatballs

Serve over hot rice, mashed potatoes or spaghetti.

1½ lbs. ground round steak
½ cup dried bread crumbs
1 egg, slightly beaten
½ cup milk
½ tsp. garlic salt

½ tsp. thyme
½ tsp. pepper
½ tsp. oregano
1 tsp. dried parsley flakes

Mix all ingredients together in a large bowl. Form meat mixture into balls, ¾ inch in diameter. Put in baking dish, 13 x 9 x 2 inches. Mix 1 package dry onion soup mix, ¼ cup water, and one 28-ounce can cheese tomato sauce. Pour onion-tomato mixture over meatballs. Bake 50 minutes in 350°-oven.

Serves 6

Swedish Meatballs

4 T. butter or margarine, divided
⅓ cup chopped onion
1 egg
1 cup milk, divided
½ cup soft bread crumbs
2½ tsp. salt, divided
3 T. sugar, divided
1 tsp. monosodium glutamate (Accent)
¼ tsp. nutmeg
1 T. dill seed
1 lb. ground beef
¼ lb. ground pork
2 T. flour
1 cup sour cream
⅛ tsp. hot sauce
1 (6-oz.) pkg. beef-flavored rice, (cooked according to directions)

Melt 2 tablespoons butter in large skillet; sauté onion until golden.

In large mixing bowl, beat egg; add ¼ cup milk and bread crumbs. Add 1¼ teaspoon salt, 2 teaspoons sugar, monosodium glutamate, nutmeg, dill, meats and sautéed onion. Blend well with fork. Form meat mixture into balls about 1¼ inches in diameter.

In skillet heat remaining 2 tablespoons butter. Drop meatballs into skillet; brown well on all sides. Remove from skillet; to fat left in skillet blend in flour, sour cream, hot sauce and remaining 1¼ teaspoon salt, 1 teaspoon sugar and ¾ cup milk. Stir over medium heat until mixture is thick and bubbly.

Return meatballs to sauce; heat thoroughly. To serve, pile meatballs in center of skillet; mound hot cooked beef-flavored rice around meatballs. Garnish with fresh dill or parsley.

Serves 4-6

Tamale Balls

Hot and spicy!

1 lb. hamburger
1 lb. ground pork
1 T. chili powder
1¼ cups cornmeal

2 tsp. salt
¾ cup tomato juice
4 cloves garlic, minced

Mix all ingredients and form into balls. Place the meatballs into a large frying pan. Make a sauce of two (8 ounce) cans of tomatoes, mashed, two teaspoons of salt, one tablespoon of chili powder. Pour over the meatballs in pan and simmer for 45 minutes to an hour.

Serves 8

Rice Meatballs

1 cup Minute Rice
1 lb. ground beef
1 egg, slightly beaten
2 tsp. grated onion
2 tsp. salt

⅛ tsp. marjoram
Dash of pepper
2½ cups tomato juice or
    2 (8-oz.) cans tomato sauce
    with ½ cup water
½ tsp. sugar

Combine Minute Rice (right from box) with beef, egg, onion, salt, marjoram, pepper and ½ cup of tomato juice. Mix lightly; shape mixture into 18 balls and place in skillet. Add ½ teaspoon sugar to the remaining 2 cups of tomato juice. Pour juice over meat balls in skillet. Bring mixture to a boil. Reduce heat and simmer, covered, 15 minutes, basting occasionally.

Serves 6

SPECIAL OCCASIONS WITH BEEF AND STEAK

Beef Roast

1 tsp. cayenne
1 tsp. ground cumin
6 garlic cloves, crushed
3/4 tsp. ground ginger
1 tsp. cinnamon
1 bay leaf, crushed
2 tsp. coriander
2 T. vinegar

1/2 tsp. turmeric
Salt to taste
4 lbs. beef, for roasting
2 cups boiling water
1 T. shortening
1 medium onion, finely sliced

Combine all ingredients except meat, shortening, onions and water. Mix to a paste. Prick meat all over with fork or skewer. Rub meat with spice paste. Set aside for 2 hours. Roast in slow oven (275°) for 3 hours. Remove meat and slice. Reserve the gravy. Melt vegetable shortening in large skillet. Add onions, fry till crisp. Add meat slices. Cover with reserved gravy. Simmer for 5 minutes.

Serves 8-10

Coffee-Flavored Pot Roast

1 pkg. instant meat marinade
2/3 cup coffee (cold)
1 clove garlic, minced
1/4 tsp. sweet basil

3 to 4 lbs. beef pot roast
1 can cream of mushroom
  soup
1 large onion, sliced

Pour contents of package of marinade into Dutch oven with tight-fitting lid. Add coffee, blend thoroughly, blend in garlic and basil. Place meat in marinade. Pierce all surfaces of meat deeply and thoroughly with fork. Marinate 15 minutes, turning serveral times. Add soup and onion; blend with marinade. Cook over low heat, turning meat once. When liquid begins to bubble, reduce heat. Cover tightly; simmer until tender, approximately 2 to 2 1/2 hours. Remove meat to hot platter. Thicken gravy if desired.

Serves 6-8

Pepper Steak

1 (1-lb.) chuck steak, cut into
   thin strips
¼ cup oil
1 clove garlic, minced
1 T. soy sauce
1 tsp. salt
1¼ cups water, divided

1 cup chopped green pepper
1 cup chopped onion
½ cup chopped celery
2-3 T. cornstarch
2 tomatoes, cut in wedges
Hot cooked rice

Brown steak in hot oil; add garlic and cook about 3 minutes. Add soy sauce, salt, and ¼ cup water; cover and cook 45 minutes. Add all vegetables, except tomatoes, and cook 10 minutes.

Combine cornstarch and 1 cup water; stir into steak mixture. Cook until slightly thick. Add tomatoes, and cook 5 additional minutes. Serve over rice.

Serves 6

Family Swiss Steak

1 (2 to 2½ lb.) chuck steak
4 T. flour
2 T. oil
1 cup chopped onion
1 cup chopped celery

1 (8-oz.) can tomato sauce
1 cup water
1½ tsp. marjoram
¼ tsp. pepper

Dredge steak with flour; brown in hot oil in a heavy skillet or Dutch oven. Remove steak and set aside.

Sauté onion and celery until soft; stir in remaining ingredients. Return steak to skillet; cover and simmer 2 hours or until meat is very tender. Remove steak to hot platter; skim fat from gravy. Heat gravy to boiling, and serve with steak.

Serves 4

Chuck Roast Steak

1 (5-lb.) chuck roast
½ cup oil
½ cup wine vinegar
½ cup catsup

1 tsp. salt
1 tsp. pepper
1 clove garlic, minced

Punch holes in roast with ice pick or knife; place in a glass dish or enamel pan.

Make a marinade by combining remaining ingredients; pour over roast. Cover and place in refrigerator at least 12 hours. Cook on grill 30 minutes for each side, basting with marinade. Reduce cooking time if medium-rare meat is desired.

Serves 8-10

LIVER

Easy Liver 'n Onions

4 slices bacon
1 lb. liver, sliced
2 T. flour

1 (10-oz.) can onion soup
¼ cup chili sauce

In skillet, cook bacon until crisp; remove from pan; drain and crumble. Dust liver with flour; brown in bacon drippings. Add bacon and remaining ingredients. Cover; simmer about 30 minutes or until liver is tender. Uncover; cook for a few minutes to thicken sauce.

Serves 4-6

Liver in Sauce

Cut 1 pound liver into strips. Season ¼ cup flour with salt and pepper. Roll liver strips in mixture. Brown liver in heavy fry pan with 3 tablespoons oil. Blend the following:

1 small, coarsely diced onion
2 cups solid pack tomatoes
½ green pepper, diced

dash cloves
1 T. flour

Pour the blended mixture into the saucepan over the liver. Cook without cover until sauce thickens slightly.

Serves 4

Turkey

Choosing and cooking turkey can be baffling. To simplify both jobs, check these pointers before turkey time. Types: There are several kinds of birds to buy. Dressed, ready-to-cook, quick-frozen turkeys are the most plentiful and come packed in airtight plastic bags.

Some people prefer fresh-chilled turkeys which have never been frozen but are somewhat more expensive.

You may choose a self-basting turkey. These birds have had fat injected beneath the skin in the breast and leg areas.

Turkey hindquarters include the leg, thigh, part of the back, piece of wing, and some giblets. They are great for small families who like dark meat.

Turkey roll roasts with both light and dark meat are also available. They range in size from two to six pounds and can be purchased plain or with gravy.

Servings: The number of servings per bird depends somewhat upon the size of appetites in your family. A homemaker can plan a pound per person when selecting a whole turkey or five ounces per serving for a boneless turkey roll. This gives everyone a generous serving plus some leftovers.

Preparation: Thaw turkey in the original moisture-proof wrapping in the refrigerator. Or, you can thaw by placing the wrapped bird in a pan of cool water; change water often. (Warm or hot water will raise the temperature of the outside of the bird too quickly.)

Ready-to-cook Weight	Approximate Time in Refrigerator	Approximate Time in Water Bath
3 to 8 lbs.	1 to 2 days	3 to 5 hours
8 to 12 lbs.	1 to 2 days	5 to 7 hours
12 to 20 lbs.	2 to 3 days	7 to 9 hours

After thawing, free legs and tail from tucked position. Remove bird from bag. Remove neck and giblets. Refrigerate within 24 hours after thawing.

Turkey Roasting Chart
325°-Oven

Purchased ready-to-cook weight	Guide to total roasting time*
6 to 8 lbs.	$3\frac{1}{2}$ to 4 hrs.
8 to 12 lbs.	4 to $4\frac{1}{2}$ hrs.
12 to 16 lbs.	$4\frac{1}{2}$ to $5\frac{1}{2}$ hrs.
16 to 20 lbs.	$5\frac{1}{2}$ to $6\frac{1}{2}$ hrs.
20 to 24 lbs.	$6\frac{1}{2}$ to $7\frac{1}{2}$ hrs.

*If turkey is unstuffed, less roasting time may be required.

To Roast Whole Turkey

Preheat oven to 325°. First, rinse thawed bird; pat dry. Stuff wishbone cavity; skewer neck skin to back. Tuck wing tips behind shoulder joints. Rub salt in body cavity; lightly fill with stuffing. Push drumsticks under band of skin at tail (or tie to tail). Brush bird with melted cooking fat. Insert meat thermometer in center of inside thigh muscle, making sure bulb does not touch bone. Place turkey, breast side up, on rack in a shallow roasting pan. Cover with a loose "cap" of foil. Avoid having foil touch top or sides of the turkey.

When turkey is two-thirds done, according to chart, cut band of skin or cord at tail so heat can reach inside of thighs. Continue cooking till meat thermometer registers 185°. The thickest part of drumstick should feel very soft when pressed between fingers protected with paper toweling; the turkey's drumstick should move up and down and twist easily in socket.

To roast in covered pan:

Preheat oven to 350°. Prepare bird as above and insert meat thermometer. Place turkey, breast side up, on rack in roasting pan. Do not add water; cover pan with lid or cover tightly with foil. Roast 11 to 12-pound turkey for 3 hours. Remove cover and cut band of skin or cord. Baste turkey with pan juices and roast, uncovered, till done, about 1 hour more. The turkey will not be as attractive as in uncovered method. If a covered dark-colored roasting pan is used, the total roasting time will be shorter. Roasting time depends on the size and conformation of the bird. The meat thermometer gives a guide to doneness, 185°.

To roast in cooking bags or wrap:

Preheat oven according to manufacturer's direction. Prepare bird as above and insert meat thermometer. Be sure to coat bag or wrap with at least 1 tablespoon flour in order to prevent bursting and release of hot fats and juices. Manufacturers also recommend that holes be punctured in the top of bags as a safety precaution. Use a pan large enough to hold the entire contents of bag or wrap, and deep enough to collect any juices released during roasting. The pan will need to be at least 1½ to 2 inches deep. Read and follow manufacturer's directions for roasting, but rely on your meat thermometer for accuracy of doneness.

Fish: Good and Cheap

Since fresh fish spoils easily unless handled with care, it should be the last item bought on a list and the first item stored. When fish comes from the market, it should be wrapped in moisture-proof paper, or placed in a covered refrigerator dish, so that the odor does not penetrate other foods. It should be cooked on the same day it is bought.

If it is to be kept longer, it should be frozen hard in a home freezer cabinet or in the freezer compartment of the refrigerator, with wax paper placed between fish fillets before freezing. But it should not be stored longer than one day even though it is frozen hard.

To tell *fresh* fish, check the eyes. "Buy the fish that is looking at you" is the way it is sometimes put—to see they are bright, clear, full and moist. The flesh should be elastic, firm and moist, and it should not hold impression made by a fingernail. The gills should be red and fresh in color, not grayish.

The scales should cling tightly, the color should be lively and unfaded and the odor should be fresh and fishy, not stale and overstrong. Frozen fish should be stored in the refrigerator freezing compartment or home freezer cabinet.

VEGETABLES

Learning the Value of Vegetables

Vegetables—fresh, canned and frozen—are a prime source of certain vitamins, minerals and important roughage. Dark-green leafy vegetables and deep-yellow ones (kale, chard, collard, mustard and turnip greens, broccoli, carrots, sweet potatoes, yams, ripe tomatoes and winter squash) are rich sources of vitamin A. Vitamin A is not easily destroyed in cooking and in fact is easier for the body to use from cooked vegetables than from raw.

Raw or lightly cooked cabbage, green peppers and dark, leafy greens are excellent sources of vitamin C; potatoes cooked in their skins are a good source too. Vitamin C content is diminished when vegetables are stored too long. To save nutrients, keep these facts in mind:

1. Once vegetables have been harvested, there is a small but steady loss of both flavor and nutrients. This loss is slowed by proper storage (including refrigeration where desirable) and is much slower in root vegetables such as potatoes and carrots than it is in greens. Use highly perishable vegetables (green beans, green peas, asparagus, leafy greens) as soon as possible.

2. Peel and cut up vegetables close to cooking time. If you cut them up sooner, cover and refrigerate.

3. Wash vegetables quickly, and preferably shortly before cooking. Do not soak cut vegetables in water.

4. Cook vegetables (except when stir-frying) in a covered pot, preferably not glass. Use as little water as necessary.

5. Certain nutrients are just under the skin of vegetables. Cook appropriate vegetables, such as potatoes, in their skins and peel after cooking.

6. Do not add baking soda to vegetables to improve color; it destroys some of the nutrients.

7. Cook vegetables for the shortest time necessary. Learn to taste-test vegetables. Cook most vegetables until they are just

tender but still crisp and slightly crunchy. Green peas, beets, sweet potatoes and white potatoes, turnips and rutabagas taste best when cooked until soft.

8. If you cook green vegetables for too long at too high a temperature, you will have discolored, unpleasantly flavored vegetables and a kitchen filled with "cabbagey" odors.

Learning How to Cook Vegetables

Steaming. Steaming vegetables really brings out their subtle flavors and reduces nutrient loss to a minimum. Buy a steamer basket, the kind with a rigid base, three short legs and flexible sides so the basket can be used in pots of different dimensions. Steamer baskets are available in hardware, variety or kitchen-supply stores, but if you don't have one, you can improvise by placing a colander in a pot that fits it and covering the pot with a tight-fitting lid.

To steam vegetables, wash or scrub them, peel if you wish, slice or leave whole. Bring about 1 inch of water to a boil in a pot—just enough to almost touch the base of the steamer. Put the steamer basket in the pot and add the vegetables. Cover pot and let water boil over moderately high heat so vegetables cook in steam. Cooking times vary, but pieces of vegetable 1 inch thick will take about 10 minutes; whole potatoes or beets, 25 to 40 minutes, depending on size. (When cooking time is long, check water level; add more if needed.) Test small pieces of vegetable for doneness by eating a piece; pierce whole roots with a small knife. Remove cooked vegetables from steamer, put them into a serving dish, add butter or margarine, salt and pepper and serve.

Skillet steaming is another excellent, quick way to cook vegetables and requires nothing more than a heavy skillet with a tight-fitting lid. Wash vegetables quickly and peel if necessary. Leave whole or cut into uniform pieces. Bring about 1/2 inch of water to a boil in a skillet; add vegetables; stir for a few seconds so they heat evenly; then cover and cook over high heat until steam builds up under the lid. Lower heat to moderate and cook vegetables until tender. Carrot slices and leafy greens will take from 5 to 8 minutes; large cubes of beets or sweet potatoes, 10 to 20 minutes, depending on size and desired tenderness.

To avoid scorching, check vegetables once or twice during cooking period to make sure water has not evaporated. When vegetables are tender, drain off any remaining liquid (or serve it with the vegetables), add butter or margarine, salt and pepper or desired seasoning and serve. Omit butter if a sauce is served with vegetables.

Stir-frying is the way Oriental cooks produce those shiny crisp vegetables so beautiful to look at and good to eat. This method is especially suited to tender vegetables like zucchini, but almost any vegetable can be stir-fried if sliced thin enough, if the pan is very hot and if the vegetables are not too crowded. Wash the vegetables and peel if necessary; cut into uniform pieces, $1/4$ to $1/2$ inch thick. Heat 1 to 2 tablespoons of oil per pound of vegetables in a large heavy skillet or wok. If desired add a little minced garlic or ginger root to the hot oil, and about 10 seconds later stir in the vegetables. Continue cooking, stirring constantly, until vegetables are crisp-tender, about 4 to 6 minutes. Serve hot.

Braising. Vegetables are cooked in a little oil with little or no water added in a covered pot. Use this method for leafy greens (turnip, kale, broccoli, rabe) and other relatively tender vegetables; it requires care and careful adjustment of the heat so the vegetables cook but do not scorch.

Wash the vegetables, peel if necessary and cut into uniform, thin slices about $1/4$ to $1/2$ inch thick; leaves can be shredded or left whole. Heat about 1 tablespoon of oil per pound of vegetables in a medium-sized skillet. Add vegetables to hot oil and stir for a minute or so to heat them evenly. Cover pan, and when steam forms inside, turn heat down to low and cook until vegetables are crisp-tender, about 5 to 10 minutes. Green leaves generally require no more liquid than that which clings to the leaves after washing; hard vegetables such as carrots may require the addition of a tablespoon or two. When vegetables are crisp-tender, add salt and pepper or desired seasoning and serve.

Boiling. As a general, everyday method of cooking vegetables, forget boiling in a large amount of water; too many nutrients get lost in the water and it's too easy to overcook.

Mature roots like potatoes or beets can be steamed or boiled.

Place them, unpeeled, in a pot of cold water and bring rapidly to a boil. When vegetables are boiling, turn down the heat, cover the pot and cook until vegetables are tender when pierced with a small knife. Large potatoes and beets may take 30 to 40 minutes.

Tips About Certain Vegetables

Beets: Choose smooth, firm beets with a good, deep-red color. If beet greens are still attached, cut them off about 2 inches above the beet as soon as you can, and if they are young and fresh, cook them as you would cook any fresh greens or add them to a salad. Wrapped in plastic, beets will keep a week or more in the refrigerator. One pound serves 2. Wash beets before cooking but do not remove roots or the red color will run into the water. Steam or boil beets with skins on; peel and slice before seasoning and serving. Beets are good sliced, mixed with onion rings and oil and vinegar dressing and served ice-cold. Beets also can be peeled and cubed or shredded and cooked in a very small amount of liquid.

Broccoli: Buy fresh-smelling, firm, dark-green bunches of broccoli with tightly closed bud clusters and no tiny yellow flowers visible. Store in refrigerator wrapped in plastic and use within 5 days. One bunch (1½ to 2 lbs.) serves 4. To prepare for cooking, cut off and discard about 2 inches from the bottom of each stalk, and any large leaves. Cut off and separate the flowerets; cut large stalks either into ½ inch long pieces or into spears; wash quickly. Steamed or skillet-steamed and seasoned with butter, salt and pepper, broccoli is delicious with almost any dish.

Cabbage: Three types of cabbage are common in the United States: smooth-leaved green cabbage, crinkly-leaved savoy and deep-purple "red" cabbage. Use smooth-leaved cabbage for slaw or cooking; savoy is best braised. Red cabbage can be used raw or cooked, but avoid using it for a New England boiled dinner unless you want purple broth and anemic cabbage. Choose firm, heavy heads of red or green cabbage with fresh outer leaves. Savoy cabbage is loose-leaved and rarely feels heavy. Uncut and wrapped well, fresh cabbage will keep several weeks in the refrigerator. One pound serves 3 or 4. To prepare for cooking, discard any damaged outer leaves and rinse the cabbage. Shred the cabbage, or cut it into wedges or 1-inch-wide strips. Cabbage is best skillet-steamed or braised. *Watch the pot. Do not overcook.* Cabbage cooks very quickly and is delicious at the crisp-tender stage and a disaster one minute later.

Cauliflower: Choose crisp, firm, heavy heads of cauliflower with creamy white flowerets free of brown blotches. (Occasionally cauliflower with green flowerets can be found in some markets and is good too.) Wrapped well, cauliflower can be stored up to 1 week in the refrigerator. One medium cauliflower (about 1½ lbs.) serves 4. To prepare for cooking, remove the outer stalk leaves and cut out as much of the core as you can (this can be grated and added to coleslaw). Leave the cauliflower whole or break off the flowerets. Cauliflower may be steamed or skillet-steamed. If water is hard, add a few drops of lemon juice or vinegar to prevent discoloration.

Beans: (green, snap, pole, wax or string) Buy bright-green, blemish-free green beans. Wax beans should be a pale, almost translucent yellow. To test beans for youth, hold a pod next to your ear and squeeze one of the beans inside; bean should burst with a crisp pop. Beans can be stored, wrapped in plastic, for up to 3 days in the refrigerator. To prepare for cooking, wash them quickly and then, as most beans are bred stringless, just cut off both ends.

Beans are delicious whole or cut in 1-inch pieces, steamed or skillet-steamed and served with butter, salt and pepper.

Dried beans and peas are often used as meat substitutes, since they are a rich source of protein. Besides being wholesome and economical, they can be used in a variety of dishes.

Here are some general rules that apply to the preparation of dried beans and peas:

(1) Dried beans and peas soaked in water (usually overnight) before cooking generally look better and have a better flavor. If this water is drained off, add it to soup.

(2) Use about 3 cups water to soak 1 cup dried beans or peas. You can expect 1 cup of these dried vegetables to yield 2½ cups when cooked; 1 pound will yield about 6 cups, or about 8 servings.

(3) A speedy method for soaking is to bring water to a boil in a

heavy saucepan, add washed beans, and boil for 2 minutes. Cover; remove from heat, and let stand for 1 hour. Cook as usual. This method is equivalent to soaking for 12 hours in cold water.

Greens: The greens group includes Swiss chard, kale, collard, dandelion and mustard greens. These dark-green leafy vegetables are a specially rich source of vitamin A and should be served often, though dandelion greens are bitter and require an acquired taste. Swiss chard is mild and its tender white stalks are as delicious as the leaves.

Buy fresh-looking greens with deep-green, undamaged leaves. Two pounds serves 4. Greens should be cooked as soon after purchase as possible, but if they must be kept a day or two, store them wrapped in plastic in the refrigerator without washing. Shortly before cooking trim tough ribs and stems, and wash the greens thoroughly several times in tepid water to remove all sand and soil. Greens are best steamed or skillet-steamed in just the water that clings to the leaves; they are good stir-fried too or braised with salt pork. Cooking time for skillet-steaming is 5 to 20 minutes, depending on tenderness of leaves. Take care not to overcook.

Okra: Peak season for okra is July through October. Choose fresh green pods from 2 to 4 inches long—the smaller the better. Avoid pods that look dull, shriveled or blemished. Okra may be left in a brown paper bag and stored in the refrigerator up to one week. One pound serves 4. To prepare okra for cooking, wash pods quickly and trim stem ends if they seem woody. Cook okra whole or sliced. To avoid the "slimy" quality which is characteristic of moist-cooked okra, stir-fry it, batter dip and deep fry it.

Green Peas: Choose well-filled, bright-green pods that squeak when rubbed between two fingers. If pods seem to be bursting at the seams, peas are too mature. Peas are sweetest when eaten as close to picking as possible, so wrap and refrigerate them and use the same day if possible. Shell peas before cooking; two pounds yield about 2 cups shelled, and serves 4. Peas are good steamed or cooked in a pan with very little water. They also make an elegant puree.

Corn on-the-cob: Thanks to refrigerated transportation, good corn is now available almost year round. Yet it is still at its very best when eaten as soon as possible after picking. Corn connoisseurs like to have the water boiling *before* harvesting the corn! Choose full ears of corn with fresh, moist-looking husks and fat, milky kernels that spurt milk when pressed. Corn that has been husked wholly or partly before it is sold is simply not corn at its best. Plan to eat corn the day you buy it, but if it must be stored *leave the husks on,* wrap it in plastic or damp paper towels and refrigerate.

Corn can be steamed or boiled. Pull off outer husk, rub off the corn silk and drop the corn into a large pot of boiling water or place it in a steamer basket over boiling water. Cook 3 to 7 minutes (allow longer time for mature corn). Drain, serve with melted butter or margarine, salt and pepper.

Eggplant: Eggplant comes in several colors—the familiar deep purple, lavender-striped white and a beautiful egglike white favored by Orientals. Most commonly available is the deep purple eggplant; pick a heavy, firm, shiny one with a fresh green cap. Refrigerate eggplant until needed and plan to use within 4 days, though it will keep longer. One medium eggplant (about 1½ lbs.) serves 4. A few eggplant recipes call for preliminary peeling, slicing and salting to remove excess liquid, but this is rarely necessary; just wipe the eggplant with a clean damp cloth. Its mild flavor adapts to many seasonings.

About Potatoes: A good way to cook potatoes is to bake them, since the nutritional value is high, there is no preparation expense to speak of and they are desirable for leftovers. Always bake at least two more than you need for use in other recipes.

For a different taste in baked potatoes, try paring them, rinsing, drying, brushing with melted margarine or bacon fat, then baking as usual.

Or mash potatoes with salt, pepper, milk and ½ cup sliced celery sauteed in melted fat until just barely tender.

Slice raw potatoes thinly. Fry in heavy skillet over medium heat until tender. Remove from skillet and keep hot. In skillet, make about 1½ cups thin white sauce. Season with ½ teaspoon pepper, 1 teaspoon salt and ¼ teaspoon sweet basil. Add fried potatoes gently; reheat briefly.

Instead of mashed potatoes with gravy or sauce, try an Italian-style dish called polenta: Dice fine or chop about 3 medium potatoes. Put in deep heavy kettle with about 1 quart water and 2 teaspoons salt. Stir in ¾ cup cornmeal and bring to boil. Cook, covered, over low heat, stirring frequently, about 45 minutes. Turn onto buttered platter and serve instead of potatoes, rice or noodles.

Speaking of noodles, make your own for a fraction of the cost and greatly superior flavor. You can make a "carload" and store them in a large jar with a tight-fitting lid for a long time. In large bowl, beat 1 egg slightly. Add enough flour to make a very stiff dough. Knead a few times, toss on a slightly floured board and roll paper thin. Roll up like jelly roll. Cut with sharp knife in ⅛" or ¼" strips. Separate well. Dry out on the board. Store in covered jar until needed.

White Potatoes: Choose firm, smooth, clean, well-shaped potatoes with no sign of discoloration and few blemishes. Do not use potatoes that have patches of green. "Idaho" potatoes cook dry and fluffy; they are especially good for baking and frying. Use "new" potatoes with their waxy texture for eating boiled or, because they hold together well, potato salads. "All-purpose" potatoes can be boiled, steamed, scalloped, mashed, baked or fried. Store potatoes in a cool, dark, dry place. Use new potatoes within two weeks. To preserve nutrients scrub potatoes and steam, bake or boil in their skins.

Sweet Potatoes: Sweet potatoes and yams are interchangeable in recipes, although they do differ slightly. Sweet potatoes have pale golden skins and yellow flesh that is deliciously dry and mealy when cooked. Yams have pale to reddish skins, orange flesh and are moister when cooked. Choose them bright, firm, smooth-skinned and as blemish-free as possible. Sweet potatoes and yams are much more perishable than white potatoes when stored under household condition. Put them in a cool, dry, dark place and plan to use within 4 or 5 days. Allow one medium-sized sweet potato or yam per serving or half a large one; scrub well, or wash and peel before cooking. Sweet potatoes are delicious baked and served with salt, pepper, and butter.

Preserving Potatoes: If potatoes do begin to form "eyes," they can easily be salvaged. Heloise, a consumer food advisor with King Features, gives this advice:

First, as soon as I see any eyes, or growth forming on the potatoes, I pick 'em off. This helps and also keeps the potatoes from going pithy for a while.

I immediately bake 'em thoroughly in my oven *without* foil. I let them cool to the touch.

Cut each one in half, scoop out the centers with a spoon, place in mixing bowl and mash while *dry*. I use my beater for this but a potato masher will do.

I then add a *little* water (NOT milk because we are going to freeze 'em) along with a drop or two of yellow food coloring and some oleo. I add salt and ground black pepper, and now is where we start. . . . I grate some cheese on the largest part of my grater (I use lots of cheese) and some raw onions.

I dump this in the mashed potatoes and stir well with fork. Do NOT heat or use mixer or masher for this.

I fill each baked potato half shell with this goop and then freeze them.

I usually put the potatoes in a throw-away pan, cover with plastic (so I can see), and secure with a few rubber bands.

Next time I want potatoes for supper, it's a lulu just to let them thaw and rebake until thoroughly warm.

I also found that after rebaking the potatoes, and just before removing them from the oven, that if I sprinkle some Parmesan cheese (or any kind of cheese) over the top and let it melt slightly to a brown tinge, that we are back up on cloud nine again.

I call these Peking Potatoes as, when I lived in China, I learned this is the way the Chinese utilize pithy potatoes.

And if you are a garlic lover, either garlic juice or garlic salt may be added to the potato mixture before filling the shell, or it can be sprinkled on top before reheating the potatoes.

For variety, sometimes I add chopped chives, the sliced tops of little green onions or chopped pimientos. Wonderful for color and taste.

Sauerkraut: The folklore of the Pennsylvania Dutch has it that for good things to happen during the year, sauerkraut must be on the New Year's Day dinner table.

Sauerkraut is, simply, brined, fermented cabbage. You might say it's in the pickle family of foods. And, although we may associate it only with German origins, it was supposedly discovered by the Chinese in the third century B.C.

Sauerkraut is a good buy—it's nutritious, and low in calories too. Three-quarters of a cup of kraut provides about one-fourth of the vitamin C needed each day by adults. It's also a good source of calcium and phosphorous. And one cup of undrained sauerkraut contains only 33 calories.

According to the U.S. Department of Agriculture's Agricultural Marketing Service, good quality sauerkraut has a pleasant, characteristic, tart, and tangy flavor. It is crisp and firm in texture, creamy white in color, and free from specks and core material.

It is available canned and in refrigerated packages which come in different sizes to suit all sizes of families. In some areas, there is also a semi-fresh product sold from barrels or similar containers.

But before you rush out to buy your good-luck sauerkraut, decide how you're going to serve it. Either use sauerkraut as it comes from the can or package or simmer it with diced apples or onions—or both—and add brown sugar to taste. Or, serve a cold sauerkraut salad.

Sauerkraut is a natural with pork and pork products so you can use your ingenuity here, too. Cook the sauerkraut with hot dogs, pork roasts, pork chops, pork steaks, spare ribs, or ham and serve this taste combination with mashed potatoes for a hearty New Year's meal.

Or, if you prefer sandwiches, make a Reuben variation with pork sausage patties, sauerkraut, Swiss cheese, and Thousand Island dressing (if desired) on pieces of toasted rye bread.

Spinach: Choose spinach with fresh, bright-green, crisp-looking leaves. Wrap loosely in plastic and refrigerate until needed. For best flavor use within a day or two. Two pounds of spinach serves 4. To prepare for cooking, cut off roots and trim any heavy midribs on leaves. Wash leaves thoroughly in several changes of tepid water to remove all sand. Spinach is delicious steamed 5 to 7 minutes in a covered pot with just the water that clings to the leaves.

Summer Squash: Summer squash are harvested while still immature, soft-skinned and relatively small. The most common varieties are yellow crook-neck, yellow straight-neck, zucchini and scallop or pattypan. Choose firm, fresh-looking squash with glossy skin. Store in refrigerator up to 2 weeks; 1 pound serves 3 or 4. To prepare for cooking, wash squash but do not peel. They can be cooked whole, sliced in rounds or strips or grated, and are good steamed, sauteed, stir-fried, broiled or baked.

BEANS

You can take hours or minutes in the preparation of a bean dish but both methods can produce equally delicious results.

Starting with dried pea or navy beans, New England Baked Beans are a gourmet dish (if you can get them started early in the morning and be around to give them attention during their long baking).

If time is short, start with canned baked beans and add a few embellishments. In just 10 minutes of skillet cooking you've got a tasty dish.

New England Baked Beans

2 cups (1 lb.) dried peas or navy
   beans
1 medium onion, sliced
1/4 lb. salt pork, sliced
1/4 cup molasses
1-2 tsp. salt
1/2 tsp. dry mustard

Wash beans; cover with cold water. Boil 2 minutes. Remove from heat and let stand 1 hour. Simmer beans gently in the same water for 45 minutes or until they begin to soften. Put half the cooked beans in a bean pot or deep baking dish. Cover with half the onion and pork. Add remaining beans, onion and pork. Mix molasses, salt and mustard with a little hot water. Pour over the beans and add more hot water to cover beans. Cover bean pot. Bake at 250° for 6 to 7 hours. Add hot water if needed. During last hour of baking, remove the cover to let beans brown on top.

Serves 6-8

Quickie Skillet Beans

1/4 cup molasses
1 T. vinegar
1 T. prepared mustard
2 T. catsup
1 T. instant minced onion
2 (16-oz.) cans baked beans

In large skillet, combine first five ingredients. Stir in the baked beans. Cover and simmer 10 minutes, stirring occasionally.

Serves 6

Bean, Bacon, and Apple Casserole

2 cups dried navy beans
1½ tsp. salt
⅛ tsp. ground ginger

3 cups sliced tart apples
⅓ cup brown sugar, firmly
    packed
8 slices Canadian bacon

Wash beans and put in large saucepan. Cover with cold water and let soak overnight. The next day, bring beans to a brisk boil in the same water; add salt and ginger. Lower temperature and simmer until bean skins begin to split. Drain, reserving liquid.

Place half the beans in an 11 x 7 x 1½ inch baking dish. Arrange sliced apples in rows over beans. Sprinkle with brown sugar, and add remaining beans. Arrange Canadian bacon slices on top. Cover and bake at 350° for 1 hour. Remove cover and add enough reheated bean liquid to barely cover beans. Return to oven and bake until beans are tender and lightly browned.

Serves 6-8

Lima Beans

2 cups dried lima beans
2 qts. water
½ lb. sliced bacon
1 large onion, chopped

2 T. flour
2 cups canned tomatoes
Salt and pepper to taste

Wash beans and put in a large saucepan. Cover with water, and let soak overnight. Pour off this water and cover beans with 2 quarts fresh water. Bring to a boil quickly; lower temperature and simmer about 2 hours or until beans are very tender. Remove from heat; drain.

Cook bacon until crisp; remove from skillet and keep warm. Brown onion in bacon drippings; add flour and stir until mixture is smooth. Add tomatoes and drained beans; cook until mixture thickens. Season to taste with salt and pepper. Serve hot with bacon strips on top.

Serves 6-8

Lima Beans with Tomato Sauce

1 onion, chopped
1 green pepper, chopped
2 T. oil
2 cups strained cooked
  tomatoes
1 cup grated American cheese

2 cups cooked dried lima beans
½ tsp. salt
¼ tsp. pepper
1 tsp. Worcestershire sauce

Sauté onion and pepper in oil. Add tomatoes and simmer 10 minutes. Add beans and seasoning and cook 20 minutes. Place beans and cheese in greased casserole and bake at 350° for 20 minutes.

Serves 4

Buckaroo Beans

1 lb. dried red beans or pinto
  beans
½ lb. smoked ham, bacon, or
  salt pork, cut in pieces
2 cloves garlic, minced
1 large onion, coarsely
  chopped
1 small bay leaf

½ cup chopped green pepper
2 tsp. chili powder
2 T. brown sugar
½ tsp. dry mustard
½ tsp. crushed oregano leaves
2 cups canned tomatoes
Salt to taste

Wash beans thoroughly in several changes of water. Put beans in a 3-quart Dutch oven, and cover with water. Let soak overnight.

The next day, add ham, garlic, onion, and bay leaf; bring to boiling point. Reduce heat; cover and simmer for 1 to 1½ hours or until beans are almost tender. Add remaining ingredients except salt. Allow to simmer, covered, for 2 hours; stir once or twice. Add salt, if needed.

Serves 8-10

Baked Beans

1 can of pork and beans
2 T. brown sugar
¼ cup catsup

Salt and pepper
2 slices bacon
  (cut in 1-inch strips)

Bake in a covered greased casserole in a 300°-oven about 1½ hours.

Serves 4

Green Bean Casserole

Drain 1 can of green beans.
Add 1 can mushroom soup.
Heat in oven about 15 or 20 minutes.
Sprinkle onion rings on top and heat about 5 more minutes.
(Canned onion rings may be used.)

Serves 4

CARROTS

Sweet and Sour Carrots

5 cups sliced carrots
1 (10¾-oz.) can cream of
   tomato soup, undiluted
½ cup oil
1 cup sugar

¾ cup vinegar
1 T. prepared mustard
1 medium onion, chopped
1 medium green pepper,
   chopped
Dash Worcestershire sauce

Cook carrots in salted water until tender; drain and set aside. Combine remaining ingredients, and cook until onion and pepper are tender; add carrots. Place in a covered dish or jar and chill overnight.

Serves 10

Company Carrot Loaf

Blend in blender until smooth:
2 cups milk
4 T. butter
½ T. cornstarch

½ tsp. salt
1½ tsp. sugar
Add:
3 cups sliced, cooked carrots
4 eggs

Blend for two seconds in blender, and pour into greased 1-quart size baking dish. Bake 1 hour at 350°.

Serves 6

Candy Carrots

Scrape 1 pound carrots and cook until tender. Drain. Melt ½ cup margarine in heavy skillet and add ½ cup brown sugar and sprinkle of cinnamon. Stir until melted. Add carrots and cook, turning, until carrots are glazed.

Serves 6

POTATOES

Scalloped Potatoes

6 medium potatoes
2 large onions
Salt and pepper
2 T. flour

2 T. butter or margarine
2 cups reconstituted instant
   nonfat dry milk
   (approximately)

Wash, peel and cut potatoes into thin slices. Peel and slice onions into thin slices. Alternate layers of potatoes and onions in a large greased baking dish. Sprinkle each layer with salt, pepper and flour. Pour in milk until it comes just to top layer; dot with butter or margarine. Cover and bake in a 325°-oven for 1 hour. Uncover and bake 1 hour longer or until tender and browned.

Serves 6

Potatoes Elegante

Cook 4 potatoes, pared and quartered, in boiling salted water until water is absorbed. Add 2 tablespoons butter and 1/2 cup milk and continue cooking until almost dry.

Blend 1 egg in electric blender. Stop blender, add 1/2 of the potato mixture and blend for 1 minute. Transfer to greased pie plate. Repeat procedure with a second egg and the remainder of the potatoes. Bake 10 minutes at 400°.

Serves 4

Potato Pancakes

Serve hot with applesauce or sour cream.

Cube 2 large peeled potatoes. Using 1/3 of the potato cubes at a time, blend for 15 seconds until grated. Remove to sieve, and drain while remainder is blended. Mix grated sieved potatoes with two eggs beaten slightly, 1 teaspoon salt, 2 tablespoons flour.

Heat oil in skillet, 1/2-inch depth. Drop the grated potato mixture by tablespoons into the hot oil. Brown on both sides. Remove and place on absorbent paper to drain.

Serves 4

Oven French Fries

4 medium potatoes
1 T. oil

$\frac{1}{2}$ cup melted butter
Salt

Peel potatoes and cut lengthwise. Soak potatoes in cold water $\frac{1}{2}$ hour, drain, then dry with paper towel. Place in a greased shallow baking pan, brush well with melted butter, and bake in 450°-oven until lightly browned (about 30 minutes), turning occasionally. Season with salt and serve.

Serves 4

Potato Puffs

$1\frac{1}{4}$ cups water
$\frac{1}{2}$ cup milk
1 envelope instant mashed potato
$\frac{1}{2}$ tsp. salt
$\frac{1}{4}$ cup grated Cheddar cheese

2 T. Parmesan cheese
2 T. butter
$\frac{1}{2}$ cup fine, dry bread crumbs
$1\frac{1}{2}$ T. melted butter
1 egg, beaten
1 T. water

Heat water and milk just to boiling; whip in instant potato, salt, cheeses, and 2 tablespoons butter. Form mixture into little balls. Mix together bread crumbs and melted butter. Roll balls in bread crumbs, then the beaten egg combined with water, and then in bread crumbs again. Arrange balls on buttered baking sheet; bake in 450°-oven for 5 minutes or until golden brown.

Serves 5-6

Yam Patties

2 T. butter
$\frac{1}{2}$ tsp. nutmeg
2 T. brown sugar

2 cups canned yams, cut
2 eggs
$\frac{2}{3}$ tsp. salt

Blend all ingredients in blender until smooth. Shape into patties and dip into $\frac{1}{2}$ cup bread crumbs. Fry in butter until light brown.

Serves 4

Speedy Sweets

Good with pot roast and green beans vinaigrette.

4 medium-sized sweet potatoes
  or yams
  (about 1½ lbs.)
3 T. butter or margarine

4 tsp. lemon juice
¾ tsp. salt
½ tsp. pepper

(Peel the potatoes and cut into 1-inch chunks.) Place potatoes in a medium-sized saucepan, cover with boiling water and then cover pan and cook potatoes over moderate heat 20 to 30 minutes. Drain off water. Add remaining ingredients and stir gently.

Serves 4

Sweet Potato Casserole

1 (17-oz.) can sweet potatoes
⅓ cup water
2 T. brown sugar
3 T. butter, melted

2 tsp. Tang orange drink
1 tsp. salt
2 T. brown sugar

Mix thoroughly sweet potatoes, water, 2 tablespoons brown sugar, butter, instant orange drink, and salt. Spoon into a 1-quart casserole. Sprinkle with remaining 2 tablespoons brown sugar. Cover; bake at 375° for 25 to 30 minutes, or until heated through.

Serves 4

OKRA

Because of its flavor and texture, okra combines well with other foods, or it can be served alone, either boiled, scalloped, pickled, or fried.

When cut into crosswise slices, the starlike shape of okra makes an attractive ingredient in casseroles, gumbos, soups, and stews. And okra packs an added bonus: it's low in calories. A half-cup serving of boiled okra contains only 36 calories.

Okra Evangeline

¾ lb. fresh okra, sliced
½ cup chopped onion
½ cup chopped ham
1 cup melted butter or
    margarine

1 cup cooked rice
Salt and pepper to taste
4 medium-size ripe tomatoes

Sauté okra, onion, and ham in butter until tender; add rice. Season with salt and pepper; set aside.

Slice off stem end of tomatoes and discard. Scoop out pulp, leaving shells intact. Stuff okra mixture into tomato shells. Bake at 400° for 10 minutes or until the tomatoes are tender.

Serves 4

Pickled Okra

Garlic (1 clove for each jar)
Hot peppers (1 for each jar)
Okra
Dill seeds (1 tsp. for each jar)

1 quart white vinegar
1 cup water
½ cup salt

Place garlic and hot pepper in hot, sterilized pint jars. Pack firmly with clean, young okra pods from which only part of the stem has been removed. Add dill seeds.

Bring vinegar, water, and salt to a boil; simmer about 5 minutes. Pour boiling-hot vinegar mixture over okra. Seal jars immediately. This amount of pickling solution will fill 5 to 7 pint jars.

Beef and Okra Casserole

1 lb. lean beef, cubed
½ cup chopped onion
¼ cup oil
2 T. flour
½ cup beef broth or canned bouillon
1 cup water
½ cup chopped green pepper
2 cups sliced carrots
2 cups sliced okra
1 tsp. salt
Dash pepper
1 tsp. Worcestershire sauce

Sauté beef and onion in oil until brown; cook slowly, stirring frequently. Blend in flour; add beef broth and water, stirring until mixture thickens. Add remaining ingredients. Cover and simmer about 1 hour, stirring frequently.

Serves 6

Southern Browned Okra

½ cup chopped onion
1 T. bacon drippings
2 cups sliced okra
3 tomatoes, peeled and sliced
1 (3-oz.) can sliced mushrooms, undrained
½ cup water
Salt and pepper to taste
Garlic powder to taste

Sauté onion in bacon drippings. Add remaining ingredients. Cover and simmer about 1 hour.

Serves 4

Okra-Tomato Casserole

2 cups sliced okra (½-in. pieces)
4 to 5 tomatoes, peeled and cut into small wedges, or 1½ cups drained canned tomatoes
1 pod green hot pepper, minced (optional)
½ cup water (omit if using canned tomatoes)
Salt and pepper to taste
1 large onion, chopped
1 T. butter or margarine

Combine all ingredients; cook over medium heat until vegetables are tender. Serve hot.

Serves 8

Okra and Tomatoes

1 lb. okra
1½ cups tomatoes, canned
½ cup oil
½ cup vinegar

3 small onions, chopped fine
1 T. parsley, chopped fine
Salt and pepper

Wash okra and cut off stems, pour vinegar over them in bowl and allow to stand for one hour. Rinse thoroughly in cold water; drain. Brown onions in hot oil then add tomatoes and cook for three minutes. Add other ingredients and bring to a quick boil. Add enough water to cover. Simmer 45 minutes.

Serves 8

Tomatoes with Okra and Peppers

12 okra pods
1 green pepper, finely chopped
¼ cup fine, dry bread crumbs
1 T. melted butter or margarine

1 tsp. minced onion
Salt and pepper
Paprika
6 medium tomatoes
Buttered bread crumbs

Wash okra and slice. Parboil 5 minutes; drain. Mix with green pepper, dry bread crumbs, butter, and onion. Season to taste with salt, pepper, and paprika.

Core tomatoes, and remove tops. Fill tomatoes with okra mixture. Place in a greased baking dish; sprinkle with buttered bread crumbs, and bake at 375° for 20 minutes.

Serves 6

BEETS

Shredded Beets

1 lb. beets
¼ cup butter or margarine
½ tsp. salt

⅛ tsp. pepper
2 T. finely chopped fresh
  parsley (optional)

Wash, peel and coarsely grate beets. Melt butter in a heavy, medium-sized skillet over moderate heat. Stir in beets, salt and pepper. Cover and cook about 15 minutes, until beets are just tender, stirring occasionally. Sprinkle with parsley and serve.

Serves 4

Harvard Beets

2 (16-oz.) cans sliced beets
½ cup cider vinegar

1 T. cornstarch
4 T. sugar

Blend cornstarch and sugar in saucepan. Add vinegar and cook over medium heat until it begins to thicken, stirring constantly. Add beets and continue stirring to prevent sticking until heated thoroughly.

Serves 8

Sweet and Sour Beets

2 (16-oz.) cans beets, drained
  (reserve juice)
2 T. flour
3 T. sugar
3 T. vinegar

1 tsp. salt
Dash celery salt
Dash of pepper
Dash of Accent

Mix flour, sugar; add vinegar and ½ cup of the beet juice. Cook, stirring constantly until shiny and smooth. Add sliced beets and seasonings and heat.

Serves 8

Idaho Beets

Drain 1 (16-oz.) can sliced beets and put in a shallow bowl. Add thinly sliced medium onion and a sliced cucumber. Pour vinegar on to just barely cover top of vegetables. Chill 1 hour.

Serves 4

GOOD GRITS, HOMINY, AND FRITTERS

Baked Grits

3 eggs
3 tsp. savor salt
1 tsp. salt
2 tsp. Tabasco sauce
1 tsp. paprika

6 cups water
1½ cups quick-cooking grits
1 lb. mild cheese (grated)
1¼ sticks butter

Beat eggs, add seasonings, and set aside. Bring 6 cups water to boil, add grits and cook until thick. Add grated cheese and butter. Let grits cool. Combine with egg mixture. Pour into buttered pan, cover and bake at 350° for 1 hour or until firm.

Serves 10

Curried Hominy Casserole

2 cups white sauce
2 cups Cheddar cheese, grated
1 tsp. curry powder

1 tsp. salt
½ tsp. white pepper
3 (20-oz.) cans white hominy, drained

Make white sauce and add cheese, curry powder, salt, and pepper. Put hominy into buttered 3-quart casserole in alternate layers with sauce. Bake at 350° for 30 minutes.

Serves 12

Vegetable Fritters

You can make fritters out of practically any cooked vegetable. Green beans, wax beans, carrots and summer squash are very good; sliced tomatoes are marvelous; even turnips are good. Drain the vegetable. Make a batter out of 1 egg, slightly beaten, ⅔ cup milk, 1 tablespoon oil, 1 cup flour and 1 teaspoon salt. (For a thinner batter, use 1 cup milk.) Dip vegetable in batter and fry in hot fat until lightly browned—about 3 minutes. Drain and serve.

Alabama Scramble

Good as part of an all-vegetable meal or with fried chicken.

¾ cup white or yellow corn meal

½ lb. white potatoes, peeled and cut into ¾-in. cubes (about 1½ cups)

½ cup oil

1¾ cups chopped onion

1 lb. fresh okra, cut into 1-in. pieces (about 4 cups)

2 green tomatoes, cut into 1-in. chunks (about 2 cups)

1 tsp. salt

¼ tsp. pepper

Place cornmeal in a paper or plastic bag; add potatoes and shake to coat with cornmeal. Remove potatoes and shake off excess cornmeal. In a heavy, 12-inch skillet heat 2 tablespoons of the oil over high heat; add potatoes and cook about 15 minutes, stirring occasionally, until evenly browned. Push potatoes to one side of skillet, heat 2 tablespoons more oil in the skillet and stir in the onion. Fry 10 minutes, stirring occasionally, until onion is golden brown. Coat okra with cornmeal as directed above. Add 2 tablespoons more oil to onion, add okra, mix in potatoes and cook 15 minutes longer, stirring occasionally. (Cooking should be done over even, high heat, but stir mixture often; adjust heat if necessary.) Coat tomatoes with cornmeal and add to skillet with remaining 2 tablespoons oil, the salt and pepper. Mix thoroughly but gently and cook 5 minutes longer, stirring once or twice.

Serves 6-8

Baked Grits II

8 cups boiling water

2 cups quick grits

1 tsp. salt

Cook until done but not dry. While hot add:

3 well-beaten eggs

2 sticks margarine

1 roll garlic cheese

2 tsp. Worcestershire sauce

1 tsp. Tabasco sauce

Put into long serving-baking dish (13 x 9 x 2-in.). Brush top with melted butter. Sprinkle paprika on top. Bake 1 hour at 300°. This is better if made one day, refrigerated, and baked the next.

Serves 12

Frontier Hominy

3 large onions, chopped
1 large green pepper, chopped
5 T. margarine, divided
1 lb. ground beef
1 (29-oz.) can hominy, drained

1/4 tsp. chili powder
1 (8-oz.) can tomato sauce
2 T. all-purpose flour
1 cup milk, scalded
3/4 cup shredded Cheddar cheese, divided

Sauté onion and pepper in 3 tablespoons margarine; add beef and cook just until pink disappears. Add hominy, chili powder, and tomato sauce. Spoon into a 2-quart casserole.

Melt 2 tablespoons margarine in a small saucepan; stir in flour, milk, and 1/2 cup cheese. Cook, stirring constantly, until cheese is melted; pour over meat mixture. Sprinkle with remaining cheese, and bake at 350° for about 35 minutes.

Serves 6-8

AN ASSORTMENT OF VEGETABLES

Midsummer Vegetable Medley

2 medium onions, thinly sliced
3 stalks celery, slivered
2 medium zucchinis, cut
2 yellow summer squash, cut
3 medium tomatoes, cut
3-4 sprigs parsley, minced
  (or 2 tsp. parsley flakes)

¼ tsp. oregano, crumbled
¼ tsp. thyme, crumbled
1 tsp. salt
⅛ tsp. pepper
¼ cup oil
½ large red and/or green
pepper, diced

To make a foil packet for the vegetables, tear off about a 2' length of heavy aluminum cooking foil (or use the lighter foil, doubled for extra strength) and turn up the sides to form a temporary pan. Slice, cut, and combine the unpeeled vegetables, except the diced pepper, which should be added at the time of serving. If the zucchini and summer squash are small, cut them crosswise into circles (no larger than 1½" across); cut medium-sized squash lengthwise and then crosswise into pieces about 1 inch wide and less than ½ inch thick. Use not-too-ripe tomatoes cut into quarters or eighths. Sprinkle herbs, salt, and pepper over the vegetables and toss lightly to mix. Add the oil. (No water is needed because celery, squash, and tomatoes have a high liquid content.) Place the ingredients in the improvised foil pan and make a packet cooking dish by holding the lengthwise edges of foil together, folding over once, and folding once again (this is known as the "pharmacy fold"). Then double or triple fold each of the two ends. The packet is now ready to be placed, folded side up, on the grill or in an oven. Cook for 30-45 minutes, depending on intensity of the fire. Unfold the lengthwise seal, add the diced peppers, and serve. In spooning out the vegetables, be careful not to pierce the bottom of the foil.

Broccoli Supreme

Frozen broccoli, canned corn, and stuffing mix make this one triply convenient.

1 slightly beaten egg
1 (10-oz.) package frozen chopped broccoli, partially thawed
1 (8½-oz.) can cream-style corn
1 T. grated onion
¼ tsp. salt
Dash pepper
3 T. butter or margarine
1 cup herb-seasoned stuffing mix

In mixing bowl, combine egg, broccoli, cream-style corn, onion, salt, and pepper. In small saucepan, melt butter or margarine; add herb-seasoned stuffing mix, tossing to coat. Stir ¾ cup of the buttered stuffing mix into vegetable mixture. Turn into ungreased 1-quart casserole. Sprinkle with remaining ¼ cup stuffing mix. Bake, uncovered, in 350°-oven for 35 to 40 minutes.

Serves 4-6

Spinach Kids Will Try

Chop 2 cups cooked spinach and add 2 well-beaten eggs, ½ cup fine cracker crumbs, ½ teaspoon salt and 3 tablespoons finely minced onion. Mix well. Drop gently by rounded spoonfuls into hot fat and fry gently.

Spinach Supreme

Defrost and cut up 1 pound frozen spinach. Blend in blender, for 3 seconds, ¼ cup Cheddar or Swiss cheese. Put aside in small bowl.

Blend for 30 seconds:
Spinach
4 eggs
1 small onion, cubed
½ tsp. salt

Melt 4 tablespoons butter in large skillet. Add spinach blend. Cook slowly, until set. Pull mixture from edge of pan. Cover top with blended cheese. Top all with ¼ cup sour cream. Place under broiler and brown lightly. Sprinkle with grated nutmeg. Serve immediately.

Serves 4

Cabbage Tamales

2 medium cabbages
1 lb. hamburger
1/2 lb. mild sausage

3 T. chili powder
Garlic
Salt to taste
1 cup River rice (uncooked)

Mix meats, rice, 1 clove garlic (minced), 1 tablespoon chili powder, and salt together. Roll mixture into small-sized tamales. (Should make about 35 to 40.) Put cabbage in hot water to wilt leaves. Cut the leaves from stem. The larger outside leaves can be cut in half for 2 tamales. Trim off hard stems in leaves if necessary. Roll leaves around tamales (separately) and secure with toothpicks. Place in heavy frying pan.

Mix 2 cans of tomato sauce with 5 cans of water. Add 2 tablespoons chili powder, salt, 1 clove garlic (minced). Pour over tamales putting toughest leaves at bottom. Turn fire high to boil, then turn low. Cover. Cook about 1 hour.

Serves 10

Cheese-Onion Bake

5 medium onions
1/4 cup butter or margarine
1/4 cup flour
2 cups milk

1/2 tsp. salt
1/8 tsp. pepper
2 cups shredded, sharp,
    process American cheese

Cut onions into thin slices; separate into rings. Place onion rings in an ungreased 1 1/2 quart casserole. Melt butter in saucepan; blend in flour, and gradually stir in milk. Cook, stirring constantly, until thickened.

Add salt, pepper, and cheese; stir until cheese has melted. Pour sauce over onions. Bake, uncovered, at 325° about 45 minutes.

Serves 6

Corn Pudding

2 cans cream-style corn
Salt and pepper
1 T. sugar

3 T. milk
4 egg yolks

Combine above in large bowl. Then beat 4 egg whites until stiff. Fold together and place in casserole. Bake in 325°-oven for 1 hour, 20 minutes.

Serves 8

Creamed-Pea Sauce

2 T. butter
2 T. flour
1 cup milk

¹/₄ tsp. salt
2 cups cooked peas

Melt butter; add flour and blend. Add milk and cook over low heat until thick, stirring constantly. Add salt and stir in cooked peas.

Fiesta Corn Bake

Serve with hot or cold cooked turkey slices.

1 (16-oz.) can cream-style corn
1 cup cooked, diced carrots
¹/₄ cup finely chopped onion
¹/₄ cup sliced, pitted, ripe olives
2 beaten eggs
1 tsp. salt

Dash pepper
Dash bottled hot pepper sauce
1³/₄ cups soft bread crumbs
   (2¹/₂ to 3 slices bread)
1 T. butter or margarine,
   melted

Combine corn, carrots, onion, and olives. Add eggs, salt, pepper, hot pepper sauce, and 1 cup of the bread crumbs; pour into 1-quart casserole. Toss the remaining ³/₄ cup crumbs with the melted butter or margarine; sprinkle atop corn mixture. Bake in moderate 350°-oven for 50 minutes. Remove from oven; let stand 5 minutes before serving. If desired, garnish with a few additional ripe olive wedges.

Serves 6

Herb-Broiled Eggplant

1 medium-sized eggplant
1/2 tsp. minced garlic
3/4 tsp. salt
1/4 tsp. pepper

1/2 tsp. dried basil or oregano
leaves
4 T. olive oil
1/4 cup finely chopped fresh
parsley

Wash and dry eggplant, trim ends and slice into 1/2-inch rounds; place on a cookie sheet. Place garlic and salt in a small bowl and mash to a smooth paste with the back of a spoon. Stir in pepper, basil, oil and 2 tablespoons of the parsley. Brush eggplant with half the herb mixture and broil 5 inches from the heat for about 8 minutes. Turn eggplant, brush with remaining herb mixture and broil 8 minutes longer, until brown and tender. Sprinkle with remaining parsley and serve hot.

Serves 4

Cabbage Casserole

Melt about 1/4 cup margarine in heavy skillet. Add 2 tablespoons flour and stir until well mixed. Add 1 (16-oz.) can tomatoes very gradually, stirring all the time and mashing tomatoes coarsely. Bring to boil, add a small head of cabbage, coarsely shredded, and 1 small onion, chopped, and season with 2 teaspoons salt and 1/4 teaspoon pepper.

SALADS, SOUPS, STEWS, AND CHILIES

SALADS

Here's a rule of thumb about salads and vegetables. Salads are good eating and excellent nutrition but you can save money without sacrificing a great deal by serving a vegetable *or* a salad when you have potatoes with a meal, and vegetable *and* a salad when you have a one-dish dinner like soup or beans.

Orange Refrigerator Salad

1 (3-oz.) pkg. orange-flavored gelatin
1 (12-oz.) carton small-curd cottage cheese
1 (11-oz.) can mandarin orange sections, drained
1 (8¼-oz.) can crushed pineapple, drained
1 (4½-oz.) carton frozen whipped topping, thawed

Sprinkle dry gelatin over cottage cheese. Add mandarin oranges and pineapple; stir gently to mix well. Fold in whipped topping. Cover and refrigerate for at least 4 hours.

Serves 8-10

Cling-a-Ling Salad

1 (3-oz.) pkg. orange flavored gelatin
1 cup boiling water
2 cups (16 oz.-can) cling peach slices
2 envelopes unflavored gelatin
½ cup lemon juice
1 (3¾-oz.) pkg. instant lemon pudding mix
1 cup salad dressing
½ cup milk

Dissolve orange gelatin in boiling water. Drain peach slices reserving ¾ cup syrup. Add syrup to gelatin; chill until thickened. Pour into 1½ quart mold. Arrange peach slices in gelatin; chill until firm.

Soften unflavored gelatin in lemon juice; stir over low heat until dissolved. Cool. Prepare pudding as directed on package; fold in salad dressing, milk and gelatin. Pour over molded peach layer. Chill until firm; unmold.

Serves 6-8

Anything Salad

Dissolve 1 (3-oz.) package lime-flavored gelatin in 2 cups hot water. Chill until slightly thickened. Add ½ cup mayonnaise and whip until well mixed. Stir in one of the following: ½ cup cottage cheese, 1 cup diced apple, ½ cup diced apple and ½ cup sliced celery, ½ cup miniature marshmallows and ½ cup finely shredded cabbage, 1 cup leftover cooked vegetables, ½ cup shredded carrot and ½ cup diced apple. Chill until firm.

Serves 4

Orange Perfection Salad

1 (3-oz.) pkg. lemon-flavored
   gelatin
2 T. sugar
¼ tsp. salt
½ cup orange juice

1 T. vinegar
1 orange, sectioned and diced
1 cup shredded cabbage
¼ cup finely chopped celery

Dissolve gelatin, sugar and salt in 1 cup boiling water. Add ½ cup cold water, the orange juice, and vinegar; chill till partially set. Fold in remaining ingredients. Chill until firm.

Serves 4

Cherry-Coke Salad

1 (16-oz.) can crushed
   pineapple
1 (16-oz.) can dark, sweet,
   pitted cherries
2 pkgs. cherry, or black
   cherry jello

2 (8-oz.) bottles, cola
   softdrink
1 cup pecans

Heat juice from cherries and pineapple, and add to jello (no water). Add remaining ingredients. Place in refrigerator until firmly set.

Serves 8

Homestead Salad

1 (10-oz.) pkg. frozen, mixed vegetables
1 (17-oz.) can red kidney beans, drained
1 cup diced celery
½ cup diced onion
½ cup chopped green pepper
¾ cup sugar
1 T. flour
1 T. prepared mustard
½ cup vinegar

Cook vegetables according to package directions; drain. Set aside to cool. Rinse kidney beans and drain well. Combine celery, onion, pepper, mixed vegetables, and kidney beans.

Combine sugar, flour, mustard, and vinegar. Cook over medium heat, stirring constantly, until clear and thick. Let cool; then stir into the vegetable mixture.

Refrigerate for 24 hours, stirring occasionally.

Serves 10-12

Green Bean Salad

1 can sliced green beans, drained
Two hard-boiled eggs, sliced
5 slices crisp bacon, crumbled
1 small onion, chopped
Stalk of celery, chopped

Mix together with salad dressing and seasoning to taste.

Serves 6

Bean Salad

1 can French-style green beans
1 can green lima beans
1 can red kidney beans
1 cup chopped celery
½ cup chopped green peppers
½ cup chopped green onions
1 cup vinegar
1 cup salad oil
2 cups sugar

Drain vegetables. Combine vinegar, sugar, oil and bring to a rolling boil—pour over the rest of the ingredients and chill overnight.

Serves 8-10

Corn Salad

⅓ cup oil
2 T. lemon juice
1 T. cider vinegar
1 clove garlic, minced
¼ tsp. salt
⅛ tsp. pepper
½ tsp. sugar
1 tsp. dried parsley flakes or 1 T. chopped fresh parsley

1 T. chopped sweet pickles or pickle relish
1 (12-oz.) can golden whole kernel corn, drained
½ tsp. salt
½ cup coarsely chopped roasted red peppers (from can or jar)
4 slices red or yellow onion, separated into rings
Bacon chips (optional)

Measure oil into a 1-cup measuring cup; add lemon juice, vinegar, garlic, the ¼ teaspoon salt, the pepper, sugar, parsley and chopped pickles; mix well. In a small bowl place the corn, the ½ teaspoon salt, the chopped red peppers and onion rings; toss to mix. Add oil and vinegar dressing to corn mixture and toss gently to coat. Salad can be served at once or chilled in freezer 10 minutes or in refrigerator for a longer period. If desired, sprinkle bacon chips over salad just before serving.

Serves 4-5

Pretty Bean Salad

1 can cut green beans
1 can cut yellow wax beans
1 small can red kidney beans

½ cup chopped onions
½ cup chopped green peppers
1 jar (or less) pimientos

Drain vegetables well and add onions, peppers, and pimientos. Marinate in:

¾ cup sugar
⅔ cup vinegar

1 tsp. salt and pepper
½ cup oil

Let set several hours, or overnight.

Serves 8

Potato and Egg Salad

6 potatoes cooked in skins
2 tsp. chopped chives
½ cup mustard French dressing
  (p. 138)

6 hard-boiled eggs
2 tsp. chopped parsley

Peel and cut potatoes in thin slices. Add sliced eggs and other ingredients. Garnish with lettuce torn in small pieces or strips of anchovies.

Serves 8

Potato-Cheese-Meat Salad

2 cups diced cooked potatoes
3 hard-cooked eggs, diced
1 cup diced celery
½ cup diced salami
½ cup diced liverwurst
½ cup diced sharp Cheddar
  cheese
1 cup finely shredded cabbage

2 tsp. instant minced onion or a
  few green onions, sliced
¼ cup olive oil
Salt and pepper
½ cup mayonnaise
Salad greens
Chopped parsley

Combine first 7 ingredients. Add onion, oil, and salt and pepper to taste. Mix lightly but thoroughly. Toss lightly with mayonnaise. Arrange greens on platter. Top with salad and sprinkle with parsley.

Serves 4-6

Potato Salad

5 medium potatoes (cooked
  and mashed)
3 hard-boiled eggs, sliced
2 T. butter
1 large onion, chopped

1 T. mustard
1 T. salad dressing (or more, to
  taste)
2 large pimientos, chopped
Salt and pepper to taste

Mix together well and chill. Add paprika if desired.

Serves 6-8

Apple-Celery Salad

Mix 2 cups diced unpeeled apple with 1 cup finely sliced celery and ½ cup mayonnaise. Sprinkle with 2 tablespoons sugar. Let stand a few minutes, then stir gently.

Serves 4

Apple-Cabbage Salad

Mix 1 cup diced unpeeled apple with 2 cups finely sliced raw cabbage. Add about ½ cup dressing made like this: Mix ¾ cup of reserved canned fruit syrup with ¼ cup vinegar and blend with about 1 tablespoon cornstarch. Cook, stirring constantly, about 2 minutes, or until mixture starts to thicken. Blend in ⅓ cup sugar, ¼ teaspoon dry mustard and 1 tablespoon margarine. Mix well; cool.

Serves 4-6

Tangy Salad

Mix 1 cup diced unpeeled apple, 1 cup finely grated carrot and 3 cups finely shredded cabbage with a dressing made like this: Beat 1 to 2 tablespoons dry mustard, depending on your taste, with 2 tablespoons evaporated milk, 2 tablespoons sugar, 2 tablespoons vinegar and ¼ teaspoon salt until fluffy.

Serves 4-6

Tuna With Peas Salad

1 (20-oz.) can peas, drained and rinsed
⅔ cup finely chopped onion
⅓ cup sliced, pitted ripe olives
1 (7-oz.) can tuna, drained and broken into large chunks
2 tsp. crushed, dried basil leaves

1 T. dried parsley flakes
½ cup olive or vegetable oil
1 tsp. dry mustard
½ tsp. salt
⅛ tsp. pepper
2 cloves garlic, minced

In a medium-sized bowl place peas, onion, olives, tuna, basil and parsley. Measure oil in a 1-cup measuring cup; add remaining ingredients and mix well. Pour dressing over tuna mixture and toss gently. Serve at once or chill if desired.

Serves 4

Hot Rice Salad

3 cups hot Herb Rice
1/4 cup minced onions
1/4 tsp. pepper
1/2 cup minced celery
1/3 cup sweet relish
2 T. minced pimientos

1/4 cup French dressing
1 tsp. salt
1/3 cup minced green peppers
1/4 cup minced sour pickle
2 hard-cooked eggs, chopped
2/3 cup mayonnaise

Combine rice, french dressing, onion, salt and pepper. Let stand while preparing remaining ingredients. Combine all and toss lightly.

Serves 6

Macaroni Ham 'n Cheese Salad

1 T. salt
3 qts. boiling water
2 cups elbow macaroni (8 oz.)
2 cups slivered, cooked ham
1 cup diced American cheese
1 cup thinly sliced celery
1/2 cup shredded carrot

2 tsp. grated onion
1/2 tsp. salt
1/4 tsp. dry mustard
1 (8-oz.) can tomato sauce
1/2 cup mayonnaise
2 T. vinegar

Add 1 tablespoon salt to rapidly boiling water. Gradually add macaroni so that water continues to boil. Cook uncovered, stirring occasionally, until tender. Drain in colander. Rinse with cold water; drain again. Combine with remaining ingredients and toss lightly; chill. Serve on crisp salad greens, if desired.

Serves 4-6

Hot Potato Salad

3½ cups (about 5) diced
   potatoes—hot
½ lb. bacon
1 onion, chopped
½ tsp. salt

¼ tsp. pepper
1 tsp. sugar
½ cup vinegar
1 egg, beaten

Cook bacon until crisp; crumble. Combine potatoes, bacon and onion. Combine ½ cup bacon drippings with remaining ingredients. Heat thoroughly, stirring constantly until thickened. Add to potato mixture and mix.

Serves 4

Hot Sweet 'n Sour Potato Salad

6 bacon slices
6 medium potatoes, cooked
   (hot)
½ cup chopped onion
⅓ cup vinegar

¼ cup Tang Instant Breakfast
   Drink
¼ cup cold water
¼ cup salad oil

Fry bacon until crisp; crumble. Peel and slice potatoes. Toss with bacon and onion. Combine vinegar, instant breakfast drink, and water in saucepan; bring to boil. Stir in salad oil. Pour over potato mixture and toss gently. Serve hot or warm.

Serves 6

Hot 'n Tangy Skillet Potato Salad

1 can condensed cream of
   celery soup
¼ cup milk
2 T. sweet pickle relish
2 T. vinegar
1 T. finely chopped onion

½ tsp. salt
Dash pepper
3 cups diced, cooked potatoes
4 or 5 frankfurters—bias sliced
   into 1-in. pieces

In medium skillet, combine soup, milk, pickle relish, vinegar, onion, salt and pepper; cook and stir till boiling. Stir in potatoes and franks; heat through. Top with snipped parsley.

Serves 6

Luncheon-Meat and Macaroni Salad

8 oz. (2 cups) elbow macaroni
Salt
1 (10-oz.) pkg. frozen peas,
  cooked and chilled
1 cup diced celery
1/2 cup sliced green onions
1 small carrot, shredded
1 medium cucumber, peeled
  and diced
1 (12-oz.) can luncheon meat,
  diced
3/4 cup to 1 cup mayonnaise
1/4 tsp. pepper
1/4 dry mustard
Lettuce (optional)

Cook macaroni in boiling salted water until tender. Drain and rinse with cold water; drain again. Add to remaining ingredients, except lettuce. Mix well and add salt to taste. Chill and serve with lettuce, if desired.

Serves 6-8

Macaroni-Fruit Salad

4 oz. (1 cup) ring macaroni
Salt
Dressing (recipe below)
3/4 cup heavy cream
1/2 tsp. vanilla extract
1 (11-oz.) can mandarin
  oranges, drained
1 1/2 cups seedless green grapes
1 (8 1/2-oz.) can pineapple
  tidbits, drained
1/2 cup miniature
  marshmallows

Cook macaroni in boiling salted water until tender. Drain and rinse with cold water; drain again. Prepare dressing, cover and cool. When ready to serve, whip cream until almost thick. Add vanilla and beat until stiff. Fold into dressing. Combine macaroni, fruits and marshmallows. Add dressing mixture and toss lightly but thoroughly.

Serves 6-8

Dressing: In top part of double boiler, combine 2 egg yolks, 1/4 cup light cream, 2 tablespoons sugar and 1 1/2 tablespoons lemon juice. Put over simmering water; cook, stirring, until thick.

Basic Coleslaw

4 cups shredded red or green
    cabbage
¼ cup chopped green pepper
¼ cup chopped onion
½ cup salad dressing

½ tsp. fennel seed (or celery
    seed)
½ tsp. salt
⅛ tsp. pepper

Toss together all ingredients. Before serving, stir in 1 cup chopped tomato or apple, if desired.

Serves 8

Mustard French Dressing

4 T. oil
4 tsp. vinegar
½ tsp. strong mustard

Salt to taste
Fresh ground pepper to taste

Mix all ingredients.

Green-Salad Dressing

In bottle with tight-fitting lid, pour ⅔ cup salad oil. Add ⅓ cup vinegar (more, if you like a tart dressing), ½ teaspoon sugar, 1 teaspoon salt, ¼ teaspoon pepper and a pinch each of marjoram, basil and oregano. Sprinkle on oregano powder. Let stand a few minutes, then shake well.

Ellen's Buttermilk Dressing

1 pint mayonnaise
1 pint buttermilk
2 T. lemon juice
1 T. Worcestershire sauce

1 T. M.S.G. (Accent)
2 T. chopped parsley
1 pkg. dressing (Italian or
    garlic)
1 tsp. salt

Mix all ingredients. Dressing keeps well in refrigerator in a tightly sealed jar. Serve on tossed green salad.

SOUPS

Cream of Potato Soup

2 cups diced, raw potatoes	4 tsp. butter
1 qt. boiling water	1 T. flour
1 pt. milk	1 tsp. salt
1 onion, chopped	Dash pepper

Cook the potato in the boiling water until soft, drain off and keep the water. Heat milk and onion in top of double boiler. Put butter in milk and let melt. Add flour, salt and pepper. Mix all ingredients together (including the potato water) and heat thoroughly.

Serves 4

Curried Chicken Soup

Sophisticated flavor with a canned soup start.

1 can condensed cream of chicken soup	1/2 tsp. curry powder
1 soup can (1 1/2 cups) milk	2 T. snipped parsley

Combine soup, milk, and curry powder; mix well. Chill several hours. Just before serving, stir in parsley; pour into well-chilled bowls. Garnish with a sprig of parsley, if desired.

Serves 4

Black Bean Soup

Blend until smooth (in blender):

1 cup drained cooked kidney beans, canned or fresh	2 T. butter
1 cup tomato juice	1/4 cup sliced onion
1 cup bean broth	1/4 cup coarsely diced celery

After blending, pour into saucepan and heat to serving temperature. May be garnished with grated hard-boiled egg yolks.

Serves 4

Split-Pea Soup

1 ham hock
1 lb. split, dry green peas
1 carrot, cut
1 slice pumpernickel
　　bread, broken
1/2 clove garlic, minced

Salt and pepper, bayleaf
1 small onion, chopped
1 stalk celery, chopped
3 qts. water
Cut ham for garnish

Put everything in a big pot. Bring to a boil, then turn heat down and simmer for an hour or two, stirring occasionally. When all is tender rub through a sieve or ricer thoroughly, to get all the pulp. Soup should be thick. Float ham cut in little pieces on top.

Serves 8

Beef Vegetable Soup

One-course dinner. Refrigerates well.

1 lb. stew meat cut in 1-in. cubes (or leftover roast)
Bone from leftover roast
1/2 cup canned corn
1/2 cup carrots, cut into 1/2-in. pieces
1/2 cup celery, cut into 1/2-in. pieces
1/2 cup onions, cut into 1/2-in. pieces
1/3 cup green pepper, cut into 1/2-in. pieces
1/2 (7 or 8 oz.) pkg. spaghetti or 1/2 cup uncooked rice
1 large potato, cut to 1-in. squares
1 (16-oz.) can tomatoes, cut to 1-in. cubes and juice

Add all or any one:

1/2 tsp. marjoram
1/2 tsp. rosemary or Italian
　　seasoning

1/2 tsp. summer savory
2 shakes Tabasco sauce

Using 4-5 quart stewer, add meat, bone, salt and pepper and 2 quarts water. Bring to boil, lower heat and cook 1-2 hours if raw meat; if leftover roast, bring to boil and add all other ingredients. Lower heat and cook until all vegetables are tender—about 1 hour. Salt and pepper to taste.

Serves 8

Bulgarian Meatball Soup

Form into meatballs and roll in flour:

1 lb. ground beef
1 cup raw rice
2 tsp. salt

1/2 cup parsley flakes
1 tsp. paprika
Pepper to taste

Soup:

4 cups water
6 chopped, green onions
1/2 chopped, green pepper
2 carrots, cut

2 cups chopped tomatoes
2 tsp. salt

Simmer 1/2 hour, covered. Add meatballs. Let come to boil, then simmer; drop in hot peppers. Let cook about 45 minutes. Mix following: 2 beaten eggs, juice of one lemon. Add some hot broth to this, then add this mixture to soup, stirring constantly. Simmer few more minutes.

Serves 4-6

Tomato Vegetable Soup

In saucepan, stir until smooth: 1 can condensed tomato soup and 1 cup broth, homemade, canned, or bouillon. In blender container place:

1/2 cup raw diced carrot
1/2 cup peeled, diced potato
1/2 cup cut celery

1/4 cup diced onion
1 cup broth, homemade, canned or bouillon

Keeping hand on cover, blend about 2 seconds, so that vegetables are coarsely shredded.

Add contents of blender container to tomato broth in saucepan. Mix and bring to boil. Simmer about 3 to 5 minutes until vegetables are tender.

Serves 4

Cream Soups

Good for leftover vegetables

Blend for 1 minute (in blender):

3 T. flour
1 tsp. salt
3 T. butter

2 tsp. Worcestershire sauce
1½ cups milk

Pour into saucepan and cook slowly. Stir until sauce thickens. Place in container and blend until smooth 1 cup sliced cooked vegetables, 1½ cups bouillon, vegetable or meat stock, or broth. Add contents of blender container to saucepan. Simmer until hot.

Serves 6

Turkey Corn Chowder

4 slices bacon, cut up
1 cup chopped onion
4 cups (1¾-lb.) cubed, pared
    potato
2 cups turkey broth
2 (10-oz.) pkg. frozen whole-
    kernel corn, thawed
¼ cup butter or margarine

2½ tsp. salt
¼ tsp. pepper
2 cups cooked turkey, cut up
    into large chunks
2 cups milk
1 cup heavy cream
2 T. chopped parsley

In 5-quart Dutch oven or heavy kettle, sauté bacon until crisp; remove; reserve. In bacon fat, sauté onion, stirring, until golden— about 5 minutes. Add potato and turkey broth. Bring to boil; simmer, covered, about 30 minutes, or just until potato is tender but not mushy. Meanwhile, in medium saucepan, combine corn, butter, salt, pepper, turkey and milk. Simmer, covered and stirring occasionally, 10 minutes. Add to potato mixture, along with the heavy cream. Cook, stirring occasionally, until hot—do not boil. Turn into warm soup tureen; sprinkle with reserved crisp bacon and chopped parsley. Serve with chowder crackers.

Serves 8-10

Hearty Chicken Soup

2 cups chicken broth*
2 cups water
1 (5⅓-oz.) can evaporated milk
2 carrots, shredded

1 envelope (5 servings) instant
  mashed potato granules
1 tsp. parsley flakes

Combine chicken broth, water, milk, and carrots in saucepan; bring to a boil. Gradually add potato granules, stirring with a fork or whisk until smooth. Stir in parsley flakes.

Serves 5-6

*Or use 1 can (10½ ozs.) condensed chicken broth and an additional ⅔ cup water.

Tuna Chowder

A quick and satisfying lunch or supper at home as well as at camp! You make it with easy-to-keep-on-hand packaged and canned foods.

1 (4-oz.) envelope green-pea
  soup mix
⅓ cup pkg. precooked rice
2 tsp. instant minced onion

3 cups cold water
1 (6½- or 7-oz.) can tuna,
  drained
Salt, pepper

In saucepan, combine green-pea soup mix, rice, and instant minced onion; stir in the cold water. Cook, stirring frequently, till mixture is boiling. Cover; simmer 3 minutes. Stir in tuna; add salt and pepper to taste. Cook till heated through.

Serves 4

Chilly-Day Soup

On a chilly, busy day, there's nothing better than a hearty, quick-fix soup for satisfying appetites.

Melt ¼ cup (½ stick) butter in a saucepan, then add ¼ cup chopped onion and 1½ cups shredded carrots. Cover and simmer 10 or 15 minutes.

Stir in 1 (10½-oz.) can condensed cream of potato soup, 2 cups milk, ½ teaspoon salt, ¼ teaspoon celery salt and pepper to taste. Heat to serving temperature and fill the bowls. Pass bread or crackers with butter.

STEWS

Browned Beef Stew

2 lbs. beef (cut in 2-in. cubes)
2 T. oil
2 tsp. salt
1/4 tsp. pepper
1/4 tsp. thyme
1/2 tsp. seasoning salt

3 bouillon cubes dissolved in 3
   cups hot water
8 small whole onions
12 small whole potatoes
6 carrots, cut in 1/2-in. slices
1 box frozen green peas

Preheat skillet to 325°. Add 2 tablespoons oil and brown beef cubes. Add bouillon, cover and simmer at 200° for about 35 minutes. Thicken with 2 tablespoons flour mixed with 1/4 cup water. Add potatoes, carrots, onions, and seasonings, and cook for 40 minutes.

Add peas about 5 minutes before stew is to be served.

Serves 6-8

Camper's Stew

What could be better camp fare or home fare than full-flavored stew? This one's especially hearty made with ground beef and served in big bowls.

1 lb. ground beef
1/2 cup chopped onion
1 can condensed beef broth
1 (16-oz.) can (2 cups) cream-
   style corn

3 large potatoes, pared and
   diced (about 3 cups)
1 tsp. salt
Dash pepper

In skillet, brown ground beef and chopped onion. Add beef broth, cream-style corn, diced potatoes, salt, and pepper; mix well. Cover; cook over low heat for 20 to 25 minutes, stirring occasionally to prevent sticking.

Serves 4

Yambilee Beef Stew

All-purpose flour
Salt
2 lbs. stew beef, cut into 1-in. cubes
1/4 cup oil
1 (10 1/2-oz.) can condensed beef broth (bouillon), undiluted
1 (8-oz.) can tomato sauce
1/3 cup chopped fresh parsley
1 clove garlic, minced
1/2 tsp. thyme leaves
1/2 tsp. pepper
1/2 bay leaf

1 large onion, chopped
12 small whole white onions
3 cloves
1/3 cup lemon juice
4 medium uncooked yams, pared and cut into 2-in. pieces (see below)
1 lb. fresh green beans, cut in half (see below)
1 cup celery pieces, about 3 stalks, cut into 1-in. pieces

Combine 1/3 cup flour and 1/2 teaspoon salt in a small bag; add meat, a few pieces at a time, and shake until evenly coated. In large Dutch oven, heat oil. Add meat and cook, a few pieces at a time, until well browned, removing pieces as they brown. Drain fat from Dutch oven.

Return meat to Dutch oven; add condensed beef broth, tomato sauce, parsley, garlic, thyme, 1 teaspoon salt, the pepper, bay leaf, and chopped onion. In one small whole white onion, place 3 cloves and add to Dutch oven; set aside remaining 11 small whole white onions. Heat to boiling. Reduce heat to low; cover and simmer 1 1/4 hours, stirring occasionally. Add lemon juice, remaining 11 small whole white onions, the yams, green beans, and celery; continue cooking for 45 minutes or more until vegetables are fork-tender.

If desired, thicken stew by removing 1/2 cup liquid from stew to a small bowl; blend in 1 tablespoon flour with the 1/2 cup liquid until smooth. Slowly stir flour mixture into stew. Stir frequently and simmer 5 minutes more or until stew is slightly thickened. Remove and discard cloves from onion. Serve stew in bowls. (Refrigerate any left over stew. Reheat slowly, stirring frequently.)

Note: Two cans (16 to 17 oz. each) yams, drained and quartered, may be substituted for fresh yams. Add during last 20 minutes of cooking time.

Two packages (9 ounces each) frozen cut green beans may be substituted for fresh beans. Add during last 20 minutes of cooking time.

Serves 8-10

Soup-Stew

Serve with corn bread and jelly.

In large kettle, break up 1 pound ground beef. Add 1 quart water, 1 (16-oz.) can tomatoes (mashed), 2 chopped onions, and 3 or 4 potatoes (cut in bite-size chunks); season with 1/2 teaspoon pepper, 1/4 teaspoon oregano, 1/4 teaspoon garlic powder and pinch of sweet basil. Simmer slowly 1 hour. Add small can whole-kernel corn, small can cut green beans and 1/2 cup regular rice. Simmer 30 minutes longer. Salt to taste (about 3 teaspoons).

Serves 4-6

Pioneer's Stew

1 cup large dry limas	1 tsp. salt
1 lb. beef stew meat, cubed	1 bay leaf
2 tsp. oil	Dash allspice
1 1/2 cups tomato juice	1 onion, quartered
1/2 cup chopped onion	3 carrots and 3 stalks celery, cut in 1-in. pieces

Soak limas in 2 1/2 cups water and 1 teaspoon salt overnight. (Or: Bring mixture to boiling; boil 2 minutes. Remove from heat; let stand 1 hour.) Coat meat with mixture of 1/4 cup flour, 1 teaspoon salt, and 1/4 teaspoon pepper, brown in hot oil. Add tomato juice, chopped onion, salt, bay leaf, and allspice. Cover; simmer 30 minutes. Add limas with liquid, and the vegetables. Cover; simmer 45 minutes, till vegetables are tender. Remove bay leaf; thicken stew, if desired.

Serves 6

Quick Skillet Stew and Dumplings

1 lb. lean ground beef
½ cup chopped onion
2 (8-oz.) cans tomato sauce
1 (10-oz.) pkg. frozen mixed
  vegetables, thawed
⅔ cup water

1 tsp. salt
½ tsp. thyme
⅛ tsp. pepper
1 cup biscuit mix
¼ cup plus 2 T. milk

Brown beef and onion in large skillet; pour off excess fat. Add 1 can tomato sauce, vegetables, water, salt, thyme and pepper. Combine well and bring to boil. Mix together biscuit mix and milk. Spoon around edge of boiling beef mixture in 5 or 6 mounds. Lower heat and simmer, uncovered, 10 minutes. Pour on remaining tomato sauce. Cover and simmer another 10 minutes.

Serves 4

Mellow Stew

¼ cup flour
1 tsp. salt
Dash pepper
2 lbs. beef stew meat, cut in 1-
  in. cubes
¼ cup oil
1 cup water

½ cup catsup
¼ cup brown sugar
¼ cup vinegar
1 T. Worcestershire sauce
1 tsp. salt
1 large onion, chopped (1 cup)
3 carrots, cut in ¾-in. pieces
  (3 cups)

Combine flour, the first teaspoon salt, and the pepper; coat meat with flour mixture. In large skillet, brown meat on all sides in hot oil. Combine water, catsup, brown sugar, vinegar, Worcestershire sauce, and the second teaspoon salt. Stir into browned meat; add onion. Cover; cook over low heat for 45 minutes, stirring once or twice. Add carrots; cook 45 minutes more or till meat and carrots are tender.

Serves 4-6

Jiffy Family Stew

Place 4 minute-steaks, one over the other, and cut into 1-inch wide strips. Mix: ¼ cup flour, ½ teaspoon salt, dash pepper, ¼ teaspoon paprika. Roll steak strips in seasoned flour. In heavy skillet melt ¼ cup butter or fat. Add meat and brown quickly, turning to brown all sides. Drain 1 pound canned new potatoes and add to skillet.

Place in blender container and blend five seconds to grate:

½ cup potato liquor or wine   1 medium diced onion
2 small diced carrots

Pour blend over stew in pan. Cover and cook 5 minutes.

Serves 4

CHILIES

Texas Chili

4 lbs. coarsely ground
  hamburger
1 lb. beef suet
4 T. chili powder
1 large onion

2 or 3 cloves garlic
1 tsp. ground cumin
½ tsp. oregano
Salt to taste
Hot water

Grind beef with coarse blade of grinder, or cut in small pieces (larger than regular ground beef).

Slice suet very thin and put into a heavy kettle or Dutch oven. Heat until you have about 3 or 4 tablespoons drippings in bottom of kettle. Remove suet and leave drippings in kettle.

Add ground beef to kettle; cook and stir until meat turns dark gray. Add chili powder and stir well. Simmer a few minutes so the meat will absorb the chili flavor. Place onion and garlic in blender and grind until smooth; add to meat-chili mixture. Add cumin and oregano. Add salt to taste; add more chili powder if desired.

Add small amounts of hot water from time to time, but chili should cook until very thick. Simmer, covered, for 2 to 3 hours.

Serves 6-8

Hearty Chili

Serve piping hot with corn bread.

Brown 1 pound hamburger, 1 cup chopped onion, 1 clove garlic, minced. Drain fat. Stir in 2 (15-ounce) cans small red beans, undrained, 1 (6-ounce) can tomato paste, 1 tablespoon chili powder, 1 teaspoon salt. Simmer, uncovered, 30 minutes.

Serves 6

Chili

1 T. salt
3 T. paprika
3 T. cumin seed
1 tsp. black pepper

½ tsp. red pepper
2 T. chili powder
½ onion, cut up fine
3 lbs. chili meat (ground beef)

150

Mix ingredients together and add ½ cup water. Bring to boil and then cook slowly 3 to 4 hours. Makes its own juice.

Serves 8-10

Sailor's Chili

It'll feed 2 dozen hungry sailors.

4 (11 oz.) cans chili-beef soup
1 (10½-oz.) can beef broth
3 (10½ oz.) soup cans water
4 (16 oz.) cans barbecued
   beans

4 (15 oz.) cans macaroni 'n
   beef in tomato sauce
1 (8-oz.) can whole-kernel corn
1 small onion, minced
Grated Parmesan cheese,
   optional

In large kettle combine all the ingredients except onion and cheese. Cook slowly, stirring until ingredients are well blended and piping hot. Garnish with minced onion and grated cheese.

NOTE: If desired, sauté onion in soup kettle with 6 strips minced bacon; drain off excess bacon fat before adding remaining ingredients. For interesting variations: add frankfurters cut in rounds or 1 can corned beef hash, slivers of green pepper, or 1 or 2 cans of kidney beans (in lieu of barbecued beans). Julienne strips of Cheddar cheese can be substituted for Parmesan cheese.

Everyone-Likes-It-Chili

2 lbs. hamburger
2 T. chili powder
1 large onion, chopped
4 T. oil

2 tsp. salt
1 clove garlic, minced
1½ qts. water
1 large can tomato paste
Cooked pinto beans, mashed

Brown meat and onion in deep pot. Add all other ingredients except beans. Simmer one hour. Add beans and cook about 10 minutes.

Serves 8

Cheese Chili

½ lb. pinto beans
5 cups canned tomatoes
1 lb. green pepper, chopped
1½ T. oil
1½ lb. onions, chopped
2 cloves garlic, crushed
½ cup parsley, chopped
½ lb. butter

3½ lbs. hamburger, fat
   removed
⅓ cup chili powder
2 T. salt
1½ tsp. pepper
1½ tsp. cumin seed
1½ tsp. M.S.G. (Accent)
1 hot dried red pepper

Wash and soak the pinto beans overnight in water. Simmer covered, in same water until beans are tender. Add tomatoes to beans and simmer 5 minutes.

Sauté green pepper in cooking oil 5 minutes. Add onions, garlic, and parsley and cook until tender, stirring often.

In a large skillet melt the butter. Add and sauté the hamburger for 15 minutes. Add meat to onion mixture. Stir in chili powder and cook for 15 minutes. Add meat to bean mixture along with salt, pepper, cumin seed and M.S.G. Simmer, covered, 1 hour. Cook uncovered for 30 minutes. At the very last of the cooking period break 1 hot dried red pepper into the chili. Sprinkle with Cheddar cheese.

Serves 10

Leftover Chili

Cut in small pieces all leftover meats—beef, ham, chicken, meat loaf. Put in saucepan with gravy or broth. Add 1 can (8 ounces) tomato sauce. Season with salt, pepper, ¼ teaspoon garlic powder, ¼ teaspoon chili powder and ¼ teaspoon oregano. Simmer gently until hot through. Heat 1 dozen flour tortillas briefly in oven, or individually on hot, dry grill. (Heat them very briefly or they will become hard and break.) Put about ¼ cup meat mixture toward one side of tortilla and roll up. Put on a platter and cover with a towel to keep warm. When all are filled, pour any remaining meat mixture over them. Serve hot with green salad and whole-kernel corn.

Serves 4-6

SPICES

Knowing and Using Spices:
The Key to Good Cheap Food

One of the best meals I have ever eaten was in a tin-roofed hut in a mountaintop construction camp for coolies in Taiwan. The food and spices in that wooden bowl of nuts, cabbage and greens were cheap. But the taste of the mixture I put into my mouth with chopsticks was rich and full. The proper blending of spices did it.

Check it out for yourself: the best dishes in French, Italian, Thai, or Greek cuisine acquire their keep-'em-coming-back-for-more tastes not so much from inclusion of esoteric, expensive ingredients but from the proper blending of spices. French soups, Italian pastas, Thai rice dishes, and Greek salads are *par excellence* because of the magic of spices.

You can do it too. Using the following chart*, you can create your own infinitely varied and zesty *good cheap food*.

*Courtesy of McCormick & Co., Inc., Baltimore, Md.

	APPETIZERS	SOUPS	SALADS AND SALAD DRESSINGS	VEGETABLES
ALLSPICE	Swedish Meat Balls, Cranberry Relish, Spiced Nuts, Pickled Eggs	Fruit Soup, Asparagus, Cream of Pea, Minestrone, Chicken, Tomato	Tomato Aspic, Fruit Salads, French Dressing, Cottage Cheese	Beets, Sweet Potatoes, Squash, Carrots, Eggplant, Spinach, Baked Beans
BASIL LEAVES	Pizza, Butter or Cream Cheese Spreads, Meat Balls, Marinated Mushrooms	Tomato, Vegetable, Lentil, Pea, Minestrone	Tomato Aspic, Tossed Green Salads, Potato, French Dressing, Herb Dressing, Sea Food, Egg	Tomatoes, Peas, Cauliflower, Potatoes, Carrots, Spinach, Eggplant, Squash
BAY LEAVES	Tomato Juice, Marinated Fish, Artichokes or Mushrooms	Chicken, Onion, Gumbo, Clam Chowder, Tomato, Vegetable, Lobster Bisque	Sea Food, Tomato Aspic, French Dressing, Herb Dressing	In Water When Cooking Most Vegetables, Pickled Beets, Rice
BON APPÉTIT	Cheese Dips, Tomato Juice, Spreads, Liver Pâté, Stuffed Celery	Vegetable, Tomato, Pea, Chicken, Lentil, Clam Chowder, Oyster Stew, Lobster Bisque	Tossed Green Salads, Sea Food, Coleslaw, Potato, Macaroni, Herb or Roquefort Dressing	Peas, Beans, Corn, Potatoes, Eggplant, Rice, Tomatoes, Squash, Turnips
CARAWAY SEED	Dips, Cheese Spreads, Cheese Straws	Borscht, Corn, Pea, Potato, Vegetable	Potato, Coleslaw, Cucumber	Sauerkraut, Cabbage, Potatoes, Cauliflower, Carrots, Squash, Beets, Beans
CARDAMON SEED	Spiced Nuts, Fruit Cocktail	Green Pea, Fruit Soup	Fruit Salads, Fruit Salad Dressings	Sweet Potatoes, Squash, Rice, Baked Beans
CAYENNE or RED PEPPER & CAYENNE	Deviled Eggs, Cheese Straws, Dips, Tomato Juice, Spreads, Guacamole	Oyster Stew, Chowders, Cream Soups, Vegetable Soup, Tomato Soup	Sea Food, Potato, Coleslaw, Macaroni, Cucumber, French Dressing, Kidney Bean	Corn, Onions, Potatoes, Asparagus, Broccoli, Eggplant
CELERY Salt, Flakes, Seed	Tomato Juice, Ham Spread, Cheese Spread, Dips, Canapés, Sauerkraut Juice	Cream of Celery, Tomato, Vegetable, Asparagus, Pea, Lentil, Oyster Stew	Tomato Aspic, Potato, Macaroni, Egg, Coleslaw, Dressing for Fruit Salads	Tomatoes, Okra, Broccoli, Sauerkraut, Asparagus, Onions, Potatoes, Corn
CHILI POWDER	Guacamole, Cheese Balls, Cheese Dips, Deviled Ham Spread	Tomato, Corn, Pepperpot, Chowders, Pea	Kidney Bean, French Dressing, Mayonnaise or Sour Cream Dressing	Corn, Eggplant, Tomatoes, Carrots, Rice, Baked Beans, Onions
CINNAMON	Broiled Grapefruit, Spiced Nuts, Cereal Nibblers, Fruit Cocktail	Fruit Soup, Tomato, Vegetable, Chicken	Mixed Fruit Salads, Waldorf Salad, Fruit Salad Dressings	Sweet Potatoes, Squash, Spinach, Asparagus, Broiled Bananas, Rice, Beets, Carrots
CLOVES	Tomato Juice, Spiced Nuts, Pickled Eggs, Cranberry Relish	Bean, Tomato, Vegetable, Pea, Clam Chowder	Tomato Aspic, Frozen Fruit Salads, Mixed Fruit Salads, Fruit Salad Dressings	Beets, Onions, Squash, Sweet Potatoes, Baked Beans, Rice, Tomatoes
CURRY POWDER	Dips, Cheese Spreads, Chicken Balls, Cereal Nibblers, Meat Balls	Mulligatawny, Curry Soup	Sea Food Salads, French Dressing, Mayonnaise or Sour Cream Dressing	Creamed Vegetables, Rice
GINGER	Broiled Grapefruit, Beef Teriyaki, Spiced Nuts, Rumaki, Spreads for Fruit or Nut Breads	Chicken, Onion, Carrot, Fish Chowders	Mixed Fruit Salads, Frozen Fruit Salads, Fruit Salad Dressings	Carrots, Squash, Sweet Potatoes, Beets, Baked Beans
HERB SEASONING	Tomato Juice, Dips, Spreads, Cocktail Pizza, Liver Pâté	Tomato, Vegetable, Lentil, Chowders, Bean, Potato	Potato, Coleslaw, Tomato Aspic, French Dressing, Herb Dressing	Eggplant, Tomatoes, Lima Beans, Broccoli, Scalloped Potatoes, Mushrooms

EGGS AND CHEESE	MEATS AND MEAT SAUCES	POULTRY AND FISH	DESSERTS & BAKED GOODS
Pickled Eggs, Cream Cheese Spreads, Spanish Omelettes, French Toast	Pot Roast, Ground Beef, Baked Ham, Stews, Tomato Sauce, Marinades, Barbecue Sauce	Creamed Chicken, Poached Fish, Spiced Shrimp	Mincemeat, Fruit Compotes, Spice Cake, Cookies, Steamed Puddings, Pie Crust, Fruit Pies
Scrambled Eggs, Cheese Spreads	Pork, Beef, Veal, Lamb, Venison, Tomato Sauce, Barbecue Sauce	Duck, Lobster, Shrimp, Chicken, Turkey, Stuffings	Herb Bread, Waffles, Croutons
Eggs Creole, Spanish Omelette, Pickled Eggs	Beef Stew, Pot Roast, Sauerbraten, Lamb Stew, Tomato Sauce, Barbecue Sauce	Stewed Chicken, Spiced Shrimp, Poached Fish, Shrimp Creole	Custard Sauce
Most Egg Dishes, Cheese Soufflé, Fondue, Cheese Sauce	Pork, Beef, Lamb, Veal, Variety Meats, Tomato Sauce, Gravies, Barbecue Sauce	Chicken, Turkey, Duck, Goose, Sea Food, Fish, Cornish Hens, Stuffings	Herb Bread, Waffles
Cottage Cheese, Omelettes, Macaroni and Cheese	Pork, Beef or Lamb Stew, Marinades for Meats	Goose, Duck, Guinea Hen, Tuna Casserole, Stuffings	Rye Bread, Waffles, Corn Bread, Biscuits, Pastry for Meat Pies, Spice Cake, Pound Cake
French Toast	Pot Roast, Pork Roast, Sauerbraten, Barbecue Sauce	Poached Fish	Cakes, Cookies, Puddings, Fruit Compotes, Custard, Danish Pastry, Coffee Cakes, Gingerbread
Cheese Soufflé, Omelettes, Macaroni and Cheese, Creamed Eggs, Welsh Rabbit, Hollandaise Sauce	Pork Chops, Pot Roast, Stews, Barbecue Sauce, Gravies	Chicken Dishes, Crab Cakes, Deviled Crab or Lobster, Turkey Pie	
Stuffed Eggs, Cheese Soufflé, Omelettes, Macaroni and Cheese, Welsh Rabbit	Pot Roast, Meat Loaf, Stews, Sauerbraten, Spiced Tongue, Tomato Sauce, Barbecue Sauce	Goose, Duck, Chicken, Turkey, Cornish Hens, Tuna Casseroles, Broiled Fish, Stuffings	Rolls, Biscuits, Dumplings
Omelettes, Soufflé, Welsh Rabbit, Stuffed Eggs	Meat Loaf, Stews, Venison, Hamburgers, Chili con Carne, Gravies, Pot Roast	Chicken with Rice, Sea Food Casseroles	Croutons
French Toast	Ham, Pork Shoulder, Boiled Beef, Pork Chops, Tomato Sauce, Barbecue Sauce	Poached Fish, Stewed Chicken, Spiced Shrimp	Cookies, Cakes, Custards, Puddings, Coffee Cakes, Stewed or Baked Fruit, Fruit Pies, Rolls, Toast
Cream Cheese Spreads, Deviled Eggs	Ham, Boiled Beef, Sauerbraten, Pork Shoulder, Pork Chops, Tomato and Barbecue Sauces, Sauce for Ham	Chicken Casseroles, Poached Fish, Spiced Shrimp, Crab Cakes, Baked Fish	Cakes, Cookies, Fruit Pies, Pastry, Sweet Rolls, Coffee Cakes, Puddings, Custards, Dessert Sauces
Egg Casseroles, Stuffed Eggs, Curried Eggs, Scrambled Eggs	Lamb, Pork, Beef, Curry Sauces	Shrimp, Lobster, Chicken, Turkey, Oysters	Fruit Compotes, Waffles, Rolls
Macaroni and Cheese, Cheese Soufflé, French Toast	Pork Roast, Pork Chops, Spareribs, Veal, Beef, Venison, Barbecue Sauce, Gravies	Roast Chicken, Chicken Casseroles, Duck, Turkey, Baked Fish, Shellfish	Gingerbread, Cakes, Cookies Toast, Fruit Compotes, Custards, Puddings, Ice Cream, Dessert Sauces
Stuffed Eggs, Macaroni and Cheese, Omelettes	Beef, Veal, Lamb, Pork, Variety Meats, Game, Gravies, Spaghetti Sauce, Barbecue Sauces	Baked Fish, Broiled Fish, Spiced Shrimp, Crab Cakes, Chicken, Stuffings	Herb Bread, Waffles, Corn Bread, Herb Croutons

	APPETIZERS	SOUPS	SALADS AND SALAD DRESSINGS	VEGETABLES
LEMON AND ORANGE PEEL	Spiced Nuts, Spreads for Fruit or Nut Breads and Cranberry Relish	Fruit Soup.	Fruit Salad Dressings, Waldorf Salad, Mixed Fruit Salads	Spinach, Carrots, Squash, Sweet Potatoes, Broccoli
MARJORAM	Meat Balls, Dips, Cocktail Pizza, Tomato Juice, Marinated Artichokes or Mushrooms	Onion, Turtle, Tomato, Vegetable, Spinach, Scotch Broth, Minestrone, Mushroom	Tomato Aspic, Tossed Green Salads, Herb Dressing	Carrots, Peas, Beans, Broccoli, Cauliflower, Brussels Sprouts, Spinach, Mushrooms, Zucchini
MUSTARD SEED OR DRY MUSTARD	Meat Balls, Dips, Ham Spreads, Tomato Juice, Pickled Eggs, Cheese Spreads	Tomato, Vegetable, Chowders, Lentil, Chicken, Potato	Coleslaw, Chicken, Potato, Macaroni, Italian Dressing, Lamaze Dressing, Mayonnaise	Asparagus, Corn, Potato, Baked Beans, Onions, Cauliflower
NUTMEG AND MACE	Eggnog, Canapés, Spiced Nuts, Meat Balls, Liver Paté	Chicken, Mushroom, Vegetable, Fruit Soup, Chowders, Oyster Stew, Split Pea, Cream of Spinach	Mixed Fruit Salads, Frozen Fruit Salads, Fruit Salad Dressings, Waldorf Salad	Spinach, Squash, Asparagus, Broccoli, Sweet Potatoes, Carrots, Green Beans
OREGANO	Meat Balls, Dips, Cocktail Pizza, Tomato Juice, Marinated Artichokes	Vegetable, Tomato, Minestrone, Onion, Chowders, Lentil	Tomato Aspic, Egg, Tuna, Salmon, Italian Dressing, Mayonnaise Dressing	Tomatoes, Carrots, Peas, Potatoes, Squash, Spinach, Beans, Turnips, Eggplant
PAPRIKA	Garnish for Canapes, Stuffed Celery, Dips, Cheese Straws	Garnish for Most Soups	Garnish for Tuna, Chicken, Egg, Macaroni or Potato Salads, French Dressing, Mayonnaise	Garnish for Potatoes, Onions, Cauliflower, Carrots, Asparagus, Creamed Vegetables
PARSLEY FLAKES	Cheese Spreads, Dips, Marinated Mushrooms or Artichokes	Garnish for Most Soups	Egg, Tuna, Chicken, Macaroni, Potato, Italian Dressing, Herb Dressing	Potatoes, Carrots, Cauliflower, Onions, Tomatoes, Eggplant, Peas, Rice
PICKLING SPICE	Marinated Mushrooms, Artichokes or Fish, Pickled Cauliflower	Beef Broth, Tomato, Vegetable	Tomato Aspic, Herb Dressing	Pickled Beets
POPPY SEED	Cheese Sticks, Dips, Spreads, Garnish		Mixed Fruit Salads, Fruit Salad Dressings	Potatoes, Noodles, Rice, Sweet Potatoes, Squash, Carrots, Asparagus, Turnips
POULTRY SEASONING	Meat Balls, Chicken Spread, Cheese Balls	Chicken, Minestrone, Lentil, Split Pea, Bean	Chicken, Turkey, SeaFood	Lima Beans, Green Beans, Eggplant, Onions
PUMPKIN PIE SPICE	Spiced Nuts, Spreads for Tea Sandwiches	Fruit Soup	Frozen Fruit Salads, Fruit Salad Dressings	Squash, Sweet Potatoes, Carrots, Rutabagas
ROSEMARY	Liver Pâté, Tomato Juice, Fruit Juice	Vegetable, Tomato, Chicken, Beef Broth, Minestrone, Pea	Tomato Aspic, Sea Food, Herb Dressing	Potatoes, Tomatoes, Cauliflower, Carrots, Lima Beans, Turnips, Green Beans, Zucchini, Brussels Sprouts, Cabbage
SAGE	Meat Balls, Chicken Spread, Cheese Balls	Minestrone, Vegetable, Tomato, Chicken, Chowders	Herb Dressing	Lima Beans, Peas, Onions, Tomatoes, Brussel Sprouts, Eggplant
SEASON-ALL	Tomato Juice, Dips, Spreads, Cheese Straws, Liver Paté, Meat Balls	Tomato, Vegetable, Corn, Onion, Chicken, Chowders, Bean	Potato, Chicken, Macaroni, Egg, Mayonnaise Dressing	Most Vegetables
SESAME SEED	Cereal Nibblers, Stuffed Mushrooms, Canapes, Cheese Balls		Tossed Green Salads, Fruit Salads, Fruit Salad Dressings	Tomatoes, Vegetable Casserole, Asparagus, Mushrooms
THYME	Liver Pâté, Cocktail Pizza, Meat Balls, Tomato Juice, Sauerkraut Juice	Vegetable, Tomato, Minestrone, Manhattan Clam Chowder, Chicken Gumbos, Bouillabaisse	Tomato Aspic, Herb Salad Dressing	Tomatoes, Onions, Brussels Sprouts, Broccoli, Lima Beans, Zucchini, Green Beans

EGGS AND CHEESE	MEATS AND MEAT SAUCES	POULTRY AND FISH	DESSERTS & BAKED GOODS
Cream Cheese Spreads, French Toast	Marinades, Pork, Veal, Ham, Stuffings, Hamburgers	Sauce for Duck Baked Fish, Broiled Fish, Duck, Chicken, Stuffings	Whipped Cream, Toppings, Dessert Sauces, Toast, Fruit Pies, Pastry, Baked or Stewed Fruit
Scrambled Eggs, Omelettes, Stuffed Eggs, Cheese Sauce, Hollandaise Sauce	Beef, Veal, Pork, Lamb, Variety Meats, Game, Tomato Sauce, Barbecue Sauce	Baked Fish, Broiled Fish, Spiced Shrimp, Crab Cakes, Chicken Dishes, Stuffings	Waffles, Herb Bread, Corn Bread, Croutons
Stuffed Eggs, Omelettes, Cheese Soufflé, Welsh Rabbit, Cheese Sauce, Creamed Eggs	Beef, Veal, Pork, Lamb, Variety Meats, Game, Tomato Sauce, Barbecue Sauce	Chicken, Turkey, Duck, Goose, Cornish Hens, Fish, Sea Food	Biscuits
Cheese Fondue, Cream Cheese Spreads, Soufflés, Creamed Eggs, French Toast, Welsh Rabbit	Hamburgers, Veal, Beef, Pork, Lamb, Gravies, Cream Sauces, Tomato Sauce, Barbecue Sauce	Chicken, Turkey, Cornish Hens, Goose, Duck, Fish, Creamed Sea Food	Doughnuts, Cakes, Cookies, Coffee Cakes, Sweet Breads, Stewed Fruit, Custards, Puddings, Dessert Sauces and Toppings
Stuffed Eggs, Omelettes, Cream Cheese Spreads, Cottage Cheese	Hamburgers, Meat Loaf, Veal, Pork, Lamb, Beef, Game, Tomato Sauce, Spaghetti Sauce	Chicken Dishes, Baked Fish, Broiled Fish, Tuna Casseroles, Stuffings	Herb Bread, Rolls, Waffles, Croutons
Garnish for Egg and Cheese Dishes	Hungarian Goulash, Veal Paprika, Garnish for Meats	Chicken Paprika, Garnish for Poultry and Fish, Excellent Browning Agent for Fried Chicken or Fish	Rolls
Scrambled Eggs, Stuffed Eggs, Omelettes, Cheese Sauces, Creamed Eggs	Pot Roast, Stews, Hamburgers, Meat Loaf, Veal Dishes, Tomato Sauces, Spaghetti Sauce	Chicken Dishes, Broiled Fish, Baked Fish, Spiced Shrimp, Stuffings, Croquettes	Biscuits, Waffles, Rolls, Dumplings
Pickled Eggs	Stews, Pot Roast, Sauerbraten, Spaghetti Sauce, Barbecue Sauce, Beef Brisket, Tongue, Marinades	Stewed Chicken, Boiled Shrimp	Stewed Fruit
Cottage Cheese, Cream Cheese, Scrambled Eggs, Omelettes, Macaroni and Cheese, French Toast	Veal and Sour Cream, Stuffing for Pork Chops	Tuna Casseroles, Chicken Casseroles, Stuffings, Chicken Livers	Danish Pastry, Cakes, Cookies, Breads, Fruit Compotes, Fillings, Dumplings
Omelettes, Scrambled Eggs	Veal Dishes, Gravies, Brown Sauce, Stews, Stuffings for Pork, Lamb or Veal, Croquettes	Chicken, Turkey, Duck, Goose, Stuffings	Waffles, Biscuits, Croutons, Dumplings
French Toast	Orange Sauce for Pork	Sauce for Duck	Pumpkin Pie, Cakes, Cookies, Coffee Cakes, Stewed Fruit, Sweet Breads, Waffles
	Stew, Lamb, Beef, Venison, Spaghetti Sauce, Barbecue Sauce, Pizza Sauce, Veal, Rabbit	Chicken Dishes, Baked Fish, Spiced Shrimp, Stuffings, Poached Fish	Herb Bread, Fruit Compotes, Corn Bread, Dumplings, Biscuits
Egg and Cheese Casseroles, Omelettes, Cheese Sauce	Stews, Pot Roast, Beef, Lamb, Pork, Venison, Gravies, Meat Loaf, Veal	Chicken, Duck, Turkey, Goose, Fish, Stuffings	Waffles, Dumplings
Most Egg and Cheese Dishes	All Meats, Most Sauces	All Poultry, All Fish or Sea Food	Herb Bread, Waffles
Cheese Spreads, Cottage Cheese, Scrambled Eggs	Steaks, Veal Dishes, Stuffings for Pork Chops, Breast of Veal or Crown Roasts	Stuffings, Fried Chicken	Cakes, Cookies, Pastry, Bread, Waffles, Biscuits, Dumplings
Spanish Omelette	Lamb, Beef, Pork, Veal, Game, Variety Meats, Liver, Gravies, Barbecue Sauces, Spaghetti Sauce	Chicken, Turkey, Duck, Goose, Baked or Broiled Fish, Spiced Shrimp, Croquettes, Stuffings	Herb Bread, Dumplings

BREADS

YEAST BREADS

Mama's Health Bread

1½ cups milk
⅓ cup corn oil
2 T. honey
2 T. molasses
2 tsp. salt
½ cup warm water
2 pkg. active dry yeast
¼ cup chopped almonds
¼ cup roasted sunflower seeds
  (shelled)

2 T. sesame seeds
2 T. wheat germ
1 T. caraway seeds
½ tsp. garlic powder
½ tsp. onion powder
2 cups unsifted rye flour
4 to 4½ cups unsifted white
  flour

Scald milk; stir in corn oil, honey, molasses and salt. Cool to lukewarm. Measure warm water into large warm bowl. Sprinkle in active dry yeast. Stir until dissolved. Add lukewarm milk mixture, almonds, sunflower seeds, sesame seeds, wheat germ, caraway seeds, garlic powder, onion powder, rye flour and 1 cup white flour. Beat until smooth.

Add enough additional flour to make a stiff dough. Turn out onto lightly floured board; knead until smooth and elastic, 8 to 10 minutes. Place in greased bowl, turning to grease top. Cover; let rise in warm place, free from draft, until doubled in bulk, about 1 hour.

Punch dough down; divide in half. Shape each piece into a loaf. Place in 2 greased 8½ x 4½ x 2½-inch loaf pans. Cover; let rise in warm place, free from draft, until doubled in bulk, about 1 hour.

Bake at 375° about 35 minutes, or until done. Remove from pans and cool on wire racks.

Makes 2 loaves

Refrigerator Bread

1 pkg. active dry yeast
²/₃ cup shortening
1 tsp. salt
1 cup scalded milk
Enough flour to make stiff dough

½ cup warm water
½ cup sugar
1 cup mashed potatoes
2 beaten eggs

Dissolve yeast in warm water. Scald milk, add shortening, sugar, salt and mashed potatoes. When cool add yeast. Mix thoroughly and add eggs. Stir in enough flour to make *stiff* dough. Turn out on slightly floured board and knead well (until dough is no longer sticky, adding more flour if needed).

Put into greased bowl large enough for it to double in size. Grease top and cover tightly with aluminum foil and place in refrigerator to rise.

This dough can be used for hot rolls baked at 425° for 15 to 20 minutes. For sweet rolls, grease muffin tins, flatten ½ the dough in bottom of pans. Sprinkle with brown sugar and pecans and place rest of dough on top. Let rise and pour cool melted butter on top. Bake at 425° for 15 to 20 minutes.

Or grease two bread pans, fill ½ full. Cover and let rise 1 hour. Bake at 325° for 45 minutes or until brown and away from sides of pan. Turn out and cool.

This dough can be kept in the refrigerator for two weeks.

Monkey Bread

3 cups flour
1 pkg. active dry yeast, dissolved in ¼ cup warm water
¼ cup shortening

½ cup milk
¼ cup sugar
1 egg
½ cup mashed potatoes
1 tsp. salt

Mix all ingredients except flour (in a blender is best). Pour into a mixing bowl. Add flour slowly. After flour mixture leaves the side of the bowl, pour dough onto floured surface. Knead slightly. Roll to ½-inch thick. Cut in 1-inch wide strips. Dip into melted butter. Place in an angel food or loaf pan. Bake 30-40 minutes at 375°. Serve hot. This makes a pull-apart ring or loaf that is great, even by itself.

Onion Bread

¾ cup milk
1 pkg. onion soup mix
½ cup sugar
½ cup soft butter

2 pkg. active dry yeast
½ cup warm water
1 egg, beaten
4 cups flour

Scald milk. Stir in onion soup mix; blend well. Stir in sugar and butter, mixing until butter melts. Cool to lukewarm. Sprinkle yeast over warm water; stir to dissolve. Add lukewarm milk mixture, egg and half the flour. Beat until smooth. Add remaining flour to make a stiff batter. Cover tightly; chill at least 2 hours. Cut dough in half. Flatten and press evenly into well-greased 1½-quart casserole. Repeat with remaining dough. Brush with melted butter or margarine. Cover with clean towel. Let rise in warm place (80°) until almost double in size. Bake in 375°-oven for about 35 minutes, or until done (bread should sound hollow when tapped.) Remove from casseroles to a rack. Brush again with melted butter or margarine. Marvelous with soups, stews, baked beans. Makes 2 loaves.

Small Family Dinner Rolls

2 T. soft shortening
1 pkg. dry yeast
1 cup warm water (not hot)
2 T. sugar

1 tsp. salt
2½ cups sifted flour
1 egg
Poppy or sesame seeds
  (optional)

Dissolve yeast in water. Stir in sugar, salt and ½ the flour. Beat until smooth. Scrape down the sides of bowl.

Seal bowl. Let rise in warm place to double-size for 45 minutes. Grease muffin tins. Punch down dough. Turn out on pastry sheet. Press dough flat, cut with cutter or shape into clover leafs. Place in tins, let rise again. Brush with melted butter. Sprinkle with seeds. Bake in preheated 400°-oven 15-20 minutes.

Makes 12 rolls

Foolproof Whole-Wheat Bread

2 T. yeast in ¹/₂ cup warm water
5 cups hot water from tap
7 cups unsifted whole-wheat
   flour
²/₃ cup honey (or molasses, or
¹/₃ cup each)

²/₃ cup oil
2 T. salt
5 to 6 cups more whole-wheat
   flour

Sprinkle yeast in ¹/₂ cup warm water. Do NOT stir. Combine 5 cups
hot tap water and 7 cups flour in mixer bowl and mix on LOW
speed, while you combine oil, salt and honey (or molasses) in a
separate bowl. Add the salt, oil and honey to the mixture in the
bread mixer and continue to mix until everything is well blended.

By this time, the yeast should have had plenty of time to brew.
The yeast should be on top of the water. Add to ingredients in the
mixing bowl and blend thoroughly. Add 5 to 6 cups of flour. Let
the dough knead on low speed for 10 minutes in heavy-duty mixer
or knead by hand for 10 minutes.

Grease three bread pans. Oil hands and the counter. Remove
dough from mixer, ¹/₃ of the amount at a time. The dough will be
sticky, but will easily form into loaves by shaping on the greased
counter.

Bake at 350° for 40 minutes. When done, remove immediately from the pans. For a softer crust, brush tops of loaves with oil
or butter. Cover with a kitchen towel to cool.

Mother's 60-Minute Hot Rolls

Dissolve 2 yeast cakes in ¹/₄ cup lukewarm water set aside. Put 1¹/₄
cups milk in a pan and add 3 tablespoons sugar, 1¹/₄ teaspoon salt
and 2 tablespoons shortening and heat to lukewarm on stove. Add
the yeast mixture.

Then add 3¹/₂ to 4 cups sifted flour. Beat until smooth and let
stand 15 minutes. Place on floured board, roll out. Cut into rolls.
Turn into greased pans and let rise 15 minutes. Bake at 450°
until golden brown.

Orange Rolls

Dissolve 2 pkgs. dry yeast in 1 cup lukewarm water.

Add:

1 tsp. salt	1/3 cup oil
1/3 cup sugar	2 eggs, beaten

Add 4 cups flour in 2 parts. Beat well until elastic. Let rise until more than doubled in bulk. Make into rolls and let rise again. Bake at 375°. Frost with orange butter, below.

Orange Butter:

Cream:
1/4 cup frozen orange juice,
    undiluted
1 1/3 sticks margarine
1 box powdered sugar

Spread on warm rolls.

QUICK BREADS

Spicy Pumpkin Bread

4 eggs, beaten
3 cups sugar
1 cup salad oil
1 (20-oz.) can pumpkin
3½ cups flour
1 tsp. baking powder
2 tsp. soda

2 tsp. salt
½ tsp. cloves
1 tsp. allspice
1 tsp. cinnamon
1 tsp. nutmeg
⅔ cup water

Combine eggs, sugar, oil, and pumpkin; mix well. Combine dry ingredients, and add to pumpkin mixture; add water, and beat well. Pour batter into 3 greased 8-inch loaf pans. Bake at 350° for 45 to 50 minutes or until a toothpick inserted in center comes out clean.

Corn Bread

1½ cups yellow cornmeal
¾ cup flour
2 tsp. baking powder

1 tsp. sugar
1 tsp. salt
1 egg

Mix all ingredients, adding enough milk for medium consistency. Prepare square pan by heating a small amount of shortening or oil in it, then sprinkle a little cornmeal on bottom and in corners of pan. Spread batter in pan and bake at 450° until done.

Hot Pepper Corn Bread

To your regular corn bread recipe add:

1 small can cream-style corn
1 small onion, chopped

½ lb. Cheddar cheese, grated
3 large Jalapeno (or other hot peppers), chopped

Mix well (mixture will be thick), pour into greased pan and bake at 450° until done.

Gingerbread

2 cups sifted flour
1 tsp. cinnamon
1/4 tsp. ginger
1 tsp. salt
1/2 tsp. nutmeg
1 1/2 tsp. baking powder

1/4 cup shortening
1/3 cup sugar
1 egg
1/2 cup molasses
1/2 cup hot water

Preheat oven to 350°. Grease and flour pan. Sift together flour, cinnamon, ginger, salt, nutmeg and baking powder. Cream shortening and sugar, beat in egg and add molasses. Add dry ingredients alternately with hot water, blending well after each addition. Pour batter into a greased 8-inch square pan. Bake 50-55 minutes or until done.

Banana-Nut Bread

1/2 cup butter or shortening
1 cup sugar
2 eggs, well beaten
2 cups sifted flour
1 tsp. vanilla

1 tsp. baking powder
1/2 tsp. soda
2 T. milk
1 1/2 cups mashed ripe banana
1/2 cup chopped nuts

Preheat oven to 350°. Cream butter and sugar, add well-beaten eggs. Add sifted flour, salt, baking powder and soda alternately with combined milk and bananas. Mix batter after each addition until smooth. Stir in chopped nuts and pour into greased loaf pan. Bake 55-60 minutes. Allow to cool before removing from pan.

Heirloom Bread

2 cups flour
1 cup sugar
1/2 cup shortening
2 eggs
1 cup applesauce

1/2 cup chopped nuts
1/2 cup raisins
1 tsp. soda
1 tsp. baking powder

Combine all ingredients and bake in 13 x 9-inch greased pan at 350° for about 45 minutes.

Green Chili Corn Bread

1/3 can drained, green chili
peppers
1 pkg. corn bread mix
1 (9-oz.) can (1 cup) cream-
style corn

2 T. bacon drippings
1 cup shredded, sharp process
American cheese

Rinse and seed peppers, cut in strips and drain on paper towels.
Prepare the mix according to directions on package. Stir in corn
and bacon drippings. Spoon half the batter in 9 x 9 x 2-inch pan.
Lay peppers over batter. Sprinkle with half the cheese. Top with
remaining batter, then cheese. Bake according to corn bread
package directions. Serve hot.

Surprising Cornmeal Muffins

2 eggs, slightly beaten
4 tsp. sugar
1 T. oil
1/2 cup self-rising flour
1/2 cup self-rising cornmeal

1/4 tsp. ground caraway seeds
1/4 cup instant nonfat dry milk
solids
1/4 cup warm water
1/4 cup shredded Cheddar
cheese

Combine eggs, sugar, and oil; stir in flour, cornmeal, and caraway
seeds.

Dissolve dry milk in warm water; add to cornmeal mixture, and
stir to mix. Add cheese; stir gently, but do not beat. Spoon into
greased 2-inch muffin pans, and bake at 375° for 10 to 12
minutes.

Makes 6 muffins

Cheese Drop Biscuits

1 cup sifted flour
1/4 tsp. salt
2 tsp. shortening

1 tsp. baking powder
2 cups grated cheese
1/2 cup milk

Sift flour, then measure. Add baking powder, salt, and sift again. Cut cheese and shortening with two knives. Add milk gradually, stirring constantly until soft dough has formed. Drop from a teaspoon onto ungreased cookie sheet. Bake at 425° for 12-15 minutes.

Makes 1 dozen biscuits

Cornmeal Pones

Blend for 2 seconds:
1 diced onion

Stop blender and add:

1 cup milk	2 eggs
1/4 cup oil or shortening	1/2 tsp. salt

Blend for 2 seconds.

Place 2 cups of white cornmeal into a mixing bowl and hollow out the center. Pour blended mixture into hollow. Mix to make a very soft dough. Shape into little cakes. Bake in 425°-oven.

Makes about 1 1/2 dozen

Hush Puppies with Onions

1 3/4 cups cornmeal	6 T. chopped onion
4 T. flour	1 egg, beaten
1 tsp. baking powder	2 cups boiling water
1 tsp. salt	Salad oil

Combine dry ingredients, onion, and egg; add boiling water, stirring constantly until mixture is smooth. Add more water if necessary. Drop by spoonfuls into deep, hot oil. Cook until golden brown.

Serves 8-10

Cranberry Muffins

2 cups sifted flour
½ cup sugar
3 tsp. baking powder
½ tsp. salt
1 cup coarsely chopped
    cranberries

1 cup milk
¼ cup butter or margarine,
    melted
2 eggs

Preheat oven to 400°. Grease 12 (2½-inch) muffin-pan cups.

Sift flour with ¼ cup sugar, the baking powder and salt into large bowl. Add ¼ cup sugar to cranberries; toss to mix. Add to flour mixture.

Measure milk in 2-cup measure. Add melted butter and the eggs; beat with fork to mix well.

Make a well in center of flour mixture. Pour in milk mixture all at once; stir quickly with fork just until dry ingredients are moistened. Do not beat. Batter will be lumpy.

Quickly dip batter into muffin-pan cups, filling two-thirds full. Bake 25 to 30 minutes, or until golden-brown.

Loosen edge of each muffin with spatula. If desired, brush tops lightly with melted butter and sprinkle with a little sugar.

Pancakes

Some people like their pancakes thick. Some like them thin. This recipe makes medium-thick pancakes. If you want your pancakes thicker, use less liquid. If you want them thinner, add more liquid. It's as simple as that!

Sift together:
1 cup sifted flour
2 tsp. baking powder
½ tsp. salt
2 tsp. sugar

Beat:
1 egg until light; add ¾ cup milk
2 T. melted shortening or oil.

Add liquid to dry ingredients, all at once; mix until well blended. Bake on hot griddle, turning only once. Serve immediately.

Makes 7 4¼-inch cakes

Cornmeal Pancakes

Prepare pancakes, decreasing flour to ³/₄ cup and adding ¹/₄ cup yellow corn meal.

Oatmeal Breakfast Pancakes

In bowl combine 1 cup sifted flour, 1 cup quick-cooking rolled oats, ¹/₂ teaspoon salt and 2¹/₂ teaspoons baking powder. With spoon, slowly beat in 1¹/₂ cup milk, then 1 egg and 2 tablespoons melted butter or margarine.

Using a ¹/₄ cup measuring cup as scoop, pour ¹/₄ cup batter onto lightly greased hot griddle. Cook until top is covered with bubbles. Turn; cook until golden.

Makes 10-12 pancakes

Toasty-Nut Granola

Serve for breakfast, instead of a bread

6 cups uncooked rolled oats
¹/₂ cup brown sugar
³/₄ cup wheat germ
¹/₂ cup flaked, shredded
  coconut
¹/₃ cup sesame seeds or
  sunflower seeds

1 cup chopped walnuts,
  pecans, peanuts, or 1 cup
  raisins
¹/₂ cup oil
¹/₃ cup honey
1¹/₂ tsp. vanilla

Heat oats in shallow baking pan in oven at 350° for about 10 minutes. Combine toasted oats, brown sugar, wheat germ, coconut, seeds and nuts. Add oil, honey, and vanilla; mix to coat dry ingredients. Divide mixture in half. Return one portion into shallow baking pan and heat at 350° 20-25 minutes, stirring every 5 minutes or so to brown evenly. Cool, then stir until crumbly. Heat the other half the same way.

Makes about 10 cups

NOTE: If you use raisins, add them after the mixture has been toasted.

DESSERTS

CAKES

Eggless Loaf Cake

1 cup sour milk
1 cup sugar
2 cups flour
1/4 tsp. salt
1 tsp. baking powder

1/2 tsp. soda
1 tsp. cinnamon
1 tsp. allspice
1 tsp. nutmeg

Mix all ingredients together. Pour into greased loaf pan. Bake at 375° for one hour or until done (toothpick inserted in center comes out clean when done).

Vanilla Wafer Cake

Cream: 2 sticks margarine
with 2 cups sugar
Add: 1/2 cup milk
6 eggs

12 oz. vanilla wafers, crushed
7 oz. coconut
1 tsp. vanilla
1 cup pecans

Mix well. Bake in loaf pan at 275° for 1 hour and 45 minutes.

Golden Loaf Cake

1 pkg. yellow cake mix
3/4 cup apricot nectar
1 (3-oz.) pkg. orange-flavored
   gelatin

4 eggs, separated
1 tsp. lemon extract

Combine first 3 ingredients. Mix well. Add egg yolks one at a time, beating after each addition. Add lemon extract. Beat egg whites until stiff but not dry; fold in. Spoon into 2 greased and floured loaf pans, 9 x 5 x 3-inches. Bake at 325° for 40 minutes, or until cake tests done. Brush on glaze, below.

Glaze:

1 cup powdered sugar
Juice of 2 lemons
Heat until sugar melts. Brush on warm cake.

Mother's Pound Cake

4 eggs (separated)
2 cups sugar
2 cups flour
1 cup milk

¾ cup shortening
1 tsp. vanilla
2 tsp. baking powder (rounded)

Cream sugar and shortening. Add egg yolks separately. Sift flour and baking powder 5 times and add to sugar mixture alternately with milk. Fold in stiffly beaten egg whites. Bake in greased and floured tube pan at 300° for 1 hour.

Chocolate Pound Cake

½ lb. butter
4 T. cocoa
3 cups flour
3 eggs
1½ tsp. vanilla

½ cup shortening
3 cups sugar
½ tsp. baking powder
1 cup milk

Separate 3 eggs; beat egg whites. Cream butter and shortening. Add sugar gradually. Add egg yolks, one at a time. Sift flour, cocoa, baking powder at least 3 times. Add flour mixture and milk alternately to above mixture. Add beaten egg whites. Cook at 325° for 1 hour and 20 minutes.

Southern Banana Cake

1 stick butter
2 cups sugar
½ cup oil
4 eggs
3 cups flour
2 tsp. soda

½ tsp. salt
2 tsp. cinnamon
1½ tsp. cloves
6 ripe bananas, mashed
1½ cups chopped nuts
1 bottle marachino cherries

Cream butter, sugar and oil. Add eggs, mix well. Add sifted dry ingredients, then bananas, cherries and nuts. Bake in greased tube pan for 1½ hours at 350°.

Sheath Cake

In a large bowl, mix and set aside:

2 cups sugar
2 cups flour

In a small saucepan bring to a boil:

2 sticks margarine
3 T. cocoa
1 cup water

Pour cocoa mixture over sugar and flour. Mix well and add:

1 egg
1 tsp. vanilla
$1/2$ tsp. cinnamon
$1/2$ cup buttermilk

Mix well and bake in well-greased 12 x 8-inch pan for 25-30 minutes at 350°. Serve with vanilla sauce (p. 185).

Cherry Pudding Cake

1¼ cups sugar
1 cup flour
1 tsp. soda
Pinch salt

1 tsp. cinnamon
1 T. melted margarine
1 egg
2 cups drained, pitted cherries

Mix all ingredients together. Pour into buttered dish, bake 45 minutes at 350°. Make sauce of the following and pour over baked pudding:

1 cup cherry juice
$1/2$ cup sugar
1½ T. cornstarch

Cook until thick. Add coloring and 1 teaspoon almond flavoring, if desired. Then add 1 T. margarine.

Holiday Cake

¼ cup butter
½ cup brown sugar (packed)
1 large egg
1 tsp. grated orange rind

¾ cup sifted cake flour
¼ tsp. salt
1 cup seedless raisins
1 lb. mixed candied fruits

Cream butter and sugar. Add egg and beat thoroughly. Blend in orange rind. Sift together flour and salt and blend in creamed mixture gradually. Rinse and dry raisins and mix with candied fruits. Add to batter. Bake in loaf pan lined with waxed paper for about 2 hours in a slow oven. Place shallow pan of water in bottom of oven.

Oatmeal Cake

Mix and set aside:

1 cup oatmeal
1½ cups boiling water

Cream well:

½ cup shortening
1 cup brown sugar
1 cup white sugar
2 eggs

1½ cups flour
½ tsp. salt
1 tsp. soda
1 tsp. cinnamon

Add oatmeal mixture to creamed mixture and blend well. Bake in greased and floured pan, 13 x 9-inch, for 30-40 minutes at 350°. Top with icing, below.

Icing:

Mix and boil 1 minute:

1 stick butter
4 T. canned milk

1 cup brown sugar

Add:

1 cup chopped pecans
1 cup coconut

Spread on hot cake and brown under broiler about 3 minutes.

180

Prune Cake

2 cups sugar
3 eggs
½ cup shortening
1½ tsp. vanilla
2 cups cooked prunes (pitted
 and chopped)
2½ cups flour
½ tsp. salt

2 tsp. cinnamon
1½ tsp. baking powder
2 tsp. soda
2 tsp. nutmeg
1 tsp. cloves
1½ cups raisins
1 cup milk
1½ cups chopped pecans

Cream sugar, shortening, eggs, vanilla, and prunes. Add sifted dry ingredients alternately with milk. Add raisins and pecans. Bake in greased tube pan for 1 hour at 350°.

Fruit Cocktail Cake

1½ cups sugar
2 cups flour
½ tsp. soda
½ tsp. salt
1 small can fruit cocktail

2 eggs, beaten
½ cup brown sugar
½ cup chopped pecans
½ cup shredded coconut

Mix sugar (white), flour, soda, and salt. Add fruit cocktail and eggs. Mix well. Pour into greased and floured 9 x 13-inch pan. Top with brown sugar, nuts, and coconut mixed together. Bake 40 minutes at 350°.

Glaze

¾ cup sugar, ½ stick butter, ½ cup milk.
Boil 2 minutes, stirring constantly. Pour over hot cake.

Lemon Ring Cake

2 cups sugar
1 cup shortening
4 eggs
1 cup milk

3 tsp. lemon extract
2½ cups flour
1 tsp. baking powder

Mix well. Bake in greased tube pan 55 minutes at 350°.

Desperation Cake

Beat 1 egg and add ½ cup sugar while beating. Add 1 cup flour mixed with 1 teaspoon baking powder and ¼ teaspoon salt. Then add ¼ cup milk, 3 tablespoons melted margarine and 1 teaspoon vanilla. Bake in greased, floured 11 x 7-inch pan in´ preheated 350°-oven for 25 minutes. Serve with Vanilla Sauce (p. 185).

Crazy Chocolate Cake

1 cup sugar	½ tsp. salt
1 egg	1 tsp. soda
½ cup sour milk	1 tsp. vanilla
½ cup cocoa	1½ cups cake flour
½ cup shortening	½ cup boiling water

Combine all ingredients in a large mixing bowl. (Do not stir until water is added.) Beat 3 minutes. Bake in 8-inch greased layer pans at 325° until done.

Quick Cherry-Angel Dessert

8 cups ½-inch cubes angel food cake	½ cups milk
1 (21-oz.) can cherry pie filling	1 cup sour cream
1 small pkg. instant vanilla pudding	

Place half of the cake pieces in a 9 x 9-inch pan. Spoon two-thirds of the cherry filling over cake. Top with remaining cake. Beat together pudding mix, milk and sour cream. Spoon over cake. Chill. Cut into 9 squares; garnish with remaining filling.

Cocoa Brownies

¾ cup sifted cake flour	½ cup shortening
¾ cup sugar	2 eggs
¼ cup cocoa	1 tsp. vanilla
½ tsp. baking powder	½ cup chopped nuts
½ tsp. salt	

Preheat oven to 350°. Sift flour, sugar, cocoa, baking powder and salt. Add shortening, eggs and vanilla. Beat 2 minutes. Add nuts and mix well. Spread batter in well greased 8-inch layer pan. Bake 30 minutes. Cool and sprinkle with powdered sugar or top with chocolate frosting.

Gingerbread Squares

½ cup shortening
½ cup sugar
1 cup molasses
2 eggs
2½ cups sifted flour
1 tsp. salt

2 tsp. baking powder
½ tsp. baking soda
1 tsp. ginger
2 tsp. cinnamon
½ tsp. cloves
1 cup hot water

Cream shortening. Gradually add sugar; cream mixture until light and fluffy. Blend in molasses. Beat in eggs, one at a time. Sift together flour, salt, baking powder, baking soda and spices. Add to creamed mixture alternately with hot water. Turn into a greased and wax paper lined 9-inch square pan. Bake at 350° 40 minutes. Cool slightly. Cut and serve with butter if desired.

Surprise Cupcakes

1¾ cups water
2 eggs
1 (18½ oz.) pkg. banana or lemon-flavored cake mix
¼ cup instant mashed potato granules
Chocolate chips, pecan or walnut halves
1 (16½-oz.) can ready-to-spread frosting

Combine water, eggs, cake mix, and potato granules in large mixer bowl. Beat at medium speed 2 minutes. Spoon into 24 greased or paper-lined muffin cups. Top each with a few chocolate chips or a nut half. Bake at 350° for 15 to 20 minutes, until cupcakes spring back when touched lightly in center. Cool and spread with frosting.

Broken Glass Cake

3 pkgs. gelatin (different colors)
1½ cups hot water (to each box)
Mix and pour separately into 3 different 8 x 8-inch cake pans.
Let above set until firm.

1¾ cup wafer crumbs
1 stick melted margarine
¼ cup sugar
Mix crumbs, margarine and sugar and line long Pyrex dish.
Save ¼ of mixture to sprinkle on top.

Mix:
1 envelope plain gelatin
3 tsp. cold water
½ pineapple juice (hot)
Let set until completely cool.

Whip 2 pkgs. whipped topping mix in 1 cup milk, add ½ cup sugar
and 1 teaspoon vanilla. Add plain gelatin mixture to the whipped
mixture. Mix well.
Cut flavored gelatins into small squares and add to whipped
mixture. Pour into lined Pyrez dish and top with the remaining
crumbs. Chill.

Buttermilk Cake

1 cup shortening	3 cups flour
3 cups sugar	1 cup buttermilk
6 eggs	1 tsp. lemon extract
¼ tsp. soda	1 tsp. vanilla

Cream shortening and sugar. Add eggs one at a time, beating well
after each addition. Add flour and soda alternately with buttermilk.
Add lemon and vanilla extract. Bake in a floured and greased tube
pan at 350° for 1 hour.

TOPPINGS

White Icing

Put 4 tablespoons flour and 1 cup milk in saucepan. Heat and stir until thick. Put in refrigerator until cold. Cream 1 cup sugar, 1/2 cup shortening and 1 tablespoon butter with 1 teaspoon vanilla. Add cooled flour mixture and beat *thoroughly*. Spread on cake.

Vanilla Sauce

Mix 1/2 cup sugar with 1 tablespoon cornstarch and add 1 cup boiling water gradually, stirring constantly. Boil 5 minutes, remove from heat and add 1 teaspoon vanilla and pinch of salt.

Syrup

Dissolve 1 cup brown sugar in 1/3 cup water, add a pinch of salt and 1/8 teaspoon cinnamon. Boil 1 minute and stir in 1/4 teaspoon vanilla. Serve on cake, pancakes or waffles.

Double-Boiler Frosting

2 egg whites	1 1/2 cups sugar
1/4 tsp. cream of tartar	1/3 cup water
1 1/2 tsp. vanilla	1 can coconut

Combine egg whites, sugar, cream of tartar and water in top of double boiler. Cook and beat with rotary beater until mixture holds shape (7 minutes). Fold in vanilla. Beat until cool and spread on cake. Sprinkle with coconut.

Chocolate Frosting

Bring to boil 1 stick margarine, 4 teaspoons cocoa, 6 teaspoons milk. Remove from heat, add one box powdered sugar, 1 teaspoon vanilla and nuts, if desired. Frosts one 9x13 inch cake.

PUDDINGS, COBBLERS, AND CUSTARDS

Jelly-Bread Pudding

8 slices white bread, crusts
    removed
3 T. soft butter or margarine
½ tsp. cinnamon
½ cup fruit preserves

3 eggs
1 (13-oz.) can evaporated milk,
    undiluted
1 T. sugar

Heat oven to 350°. Grease an 8-inch-square baking dish, preferably glass or pottery (not metal). Spread one side of each slice of bread with the butter. Place 4 slices in one layer on the bottom of the baking dish, buttered side up; sprinkle with ¼ teaspoon of the cinnamon and spread with half the preserves. Top with remaining bread, cinnamon and preserves. Beat eggs, milk and sugar in a bowl; pour over bread layers in baking dish. Place dish in the oven on a shelf just above the center and bake 50 to 60 minutes, or until nicely browned. Serve pudding warm or cold.

Serves 4-6

Cranberry-Oat Dessert

1 cup rolled oats
½ cup flour
¼ tsp. ground cinnamon
4 T. (½ stick) butter or mar-
    garine, cut into small pieces

4 T. honey
1 (16-oz.) can whole cranberry
    sauce

Heat oven to 325°. In a medium-sized bowl mix the oats, flour and cinnamon. Add butter to oat mixture and blend well. Add the honey and stir into mixture with a fork; mixture will be sticky and lumpy. Spread cranberry sauce over bottom of a shallow, 8-inch-round baking dish and spread oat mixture over it. Bake 40 minutes, or until top is lightly browned and cranberries are bubbly. Serve hot or cold.

Poor Man's Pudding

Mix 4 cups milk with 3 tablespoons regular rice, ½ teaspoon salt, ⅓ cup molasses and ½ teaspoon cinnamon. Pour into buttered casserole and bake in preheated 300°-oven about 3 hours, stirring 3 or 4 times during first hour to keep rice from settling. At last stirring, add 2 tablespoons margarine.

Quick Banana Pudding

1 pkg. vanilla instant pudding
   mix
3 medium bananas sliced

24 vanilla wafers, broken or
   crushed
½ cup toasted coconut

Prepare pudding according to directions on the package. Place alternate layers of bananas, wafers, and pudding in parfait glasses or serving dishes. Top with coconut.

Serves 6

Quick 'n Easy Vanilla Whip

1 pkg. red gelatin
1 cup hot water

1 to 1½ cup vanilla ice cream
Strawberries if desired

Mix one package of any red gelatin with 1 cup hot water. Add 1 to 1½ cups vanilla ice cream and beat till ice cream is melted. Pour into a fancy mold or serving dish and put in refrigerator till set, usually about 1 hour. A few strawberries may be added if desired.

Fruit Whip

2 egg whites
½ cup powdered sugar
1 cup fruit, chopped or crushed

Beat egg whites until stiff. Add sugar gradually while beating. Fold in fruit. Pile in sherbet glasses. Chill.

Serves 4

Apple Crisp

4 cups pared and sliced tart
  apples
2 T. sugar
¼ tsp. cinnamon
¼ cup water

½ cup flour
⅛ tsp. salt
¼ tsp. nutmeg
⅓ cup brown sugar
3 T. margarine

Mix sugar, cinnamon, and apples in a mixing bowl. Spread apples in a greased 8 x 8-inch baking pan and sprinkle with water.

Blend remaining ingredients together and spread over apples. Bake uncovered in a 325°-oven for 1 hour or until lightly browned and apples are tender.

Blueberry-Peach Cobbler

1 pkg. blueberry muffin mix
¼ cup sugar
½ tsp. cinnamon
6 T. butter or margarine
½ cup chopped pecans

2 (22-oz.) cans peach pie filling
¼ cup sugar
1 tsp. cinnamon
1 tsp. almond extract

Preheat oven to 350°. In a medium bowl combine muffin mix, ¼ cup sugar and ½ teaspoon cinnamon. Cut in butter, then stir in nuts. In a 13 x 9-inch pan combine pie filling, ¼ cup sugar, 1 teaspoon cinnamon and the almond extract. Spoon the crumb topping over the peach mixture. Bake at 350° for 35-40 minutes, until topping is golden brown. Serve with ice cream, if desired.

Cherry Cobbler

1 (21-oz.) can cherry pie filling
½ tsp. vanilla
2 cups biscuit mix

½ cup reconstituted nonfat dry
  milk
1 T. sugar

Mix pie filling and vanilla in a square pan, 8 x 8 x 2 inches. Combine biscuit mix, milk, and sugar in a bowl. Stir until dough forms a ball and cleans the bowl. Drop dough by spoonfuls over cherries. Bake in a 325°-oven 35 to 40 minutes or until golden brown. Serve warm.

Fruit Cobbler

1 cup flour
1 cup sugar
1 cup milk

1 tsp. baking powder
4 cups cooked fruit, canned or
    fresh

Make a batter of the flour, sugar, baking powder and milk. Pour into baking dish, then pour fruit over it. Bake in a moderate oven until the batter has risen to top of fruit and browned.

Quickie Cobbler

Pie Crust:
1 cup flour, ⅓ cup shortening, ⅓ cup ice water. Blend as any pastry. Roll out on floured cookie sheet and cut into strips. Bake until edges are brown—400°.
Berry Filling:
1 pkg. frozen berries and juice (enough to make 2 cups or more). Heat (strain if seeds are not desired). Add 1½ cups sugar, ¼ cup flour, mixed together, slowly to berries. It will thicken when coming to a boil.

Place crust in dish alternately with berries. Top with remaining crust. Top with whipped cream or ice cream.

Trifle

Place in a deep dish, rounds of yellow, sponge, or white cake. Soak with 1 tablespoon rum flavoring mixed with 1 tablespoon water and fruit juice—enough to saturate the cake.

Make a gelatin with water or juice (according to directions on package) and add fruit. When gelatin and fruit are partly set, pour over cake; allow to set completely.

Prepare a rich custard using vanilla, banana, coconut, etc., and pour over gelatin.

When custard is set, cover with layer of sliced bananas; top with whipped cream and garnish.

Cherry Cinammon Cobbler

1 cup sugar	1 stick margarine
1 cup flour	1 large can cherry pie filling
1 cup milk	Combine in separate bowl:
3 tsp. baking powder	2 T. cinnamon
Pinch salt	2 T. sugar

Preheat oven to 375°. Melt margarine in a baking dish. When it is melted, add the fruit without mixing. In a separate dish combine sugar, flour, baking powder, and salt. Add milk a little at a time to make a non-lumpy paste. Pour this batter over the top of the fruit, covering it completely. Bake at 375° for 45 minutes until the center of the batter is done. Remove, dust with cinnamon-sugar, return to oven immediately, for a few minutes.

Baked Apples with Soft Custard

Marvelous over baked apples, is a velvety soft custard.

For this nutritious, quick-to-fix version: combine 1 package (3¼-oz.) vanilla pudding and pie filling mix with 1 cup milk; stir until smooth; add 2 cups milk, and cook and stir over medium heat until mixture comes to a full boil.

Remove from heat. Stir in 1 teaspoon vanilla. Chill thoroughly. Serve over baked apples or fruit compote.

Caramel Custard Cups

Preheat oven to 350°.

Press 1 tablespoon brown sugar lightly into each of 4 custard cups. Mix in a 1-quart bowl 2 eggs, slightly beaten, 1 cup evaporated skimmed milk, ⅔ cup water, ⅓ cup sugar, 1½ teaspoon vanilla and a few grains of salt.

Pour carefully over brown sugar. Set cups in a shallow pan holding 1 inch of hot water. Bake 50 minutes, or until knife inserted near edge of custard comes out clean. Cool. Loosen edges with knife. Unmold.

Baked Apple Tapioca

2½ cups thickly sliced, tart apples
3 T. butter
¼ tsp. mace
½ cup quick-cooking tapioca
1 cup firmly packed, light brown sugar
¾ tsp. salt
3 cups water
1 to 2 T. lemon juice

Arrange apples in greased baking dish. Dot with butter and sprinkle with mace. Combine remaining ingredients in saucepan and mix well. Place over medium heat and cook until mixture comes to a boil, stirring constantly. Remove from heat. Pour over apples in baking dish. Cover and bake in 375°-oven 20 minutes, or until apples are tender.

Serve warm with cream.

Serves 6-8

Canned Peaches with Soft Custard

1 (16-oz.) can sliced peaches, drained
3 or 4 egg yolks, slightly beaten
¼ cup sugar
⅛ tsp. salt
2 cups milk
1 tsp. vanilla extract

Arrange peaches in 6 individual serving dishes. Place in refrigerator to chill.

Put egg yolks in top of double boiler; add sugar and salt. Scald milk and slowly add to egg mixture. (Be sure water in bottom of double boiler does not reach boiling stage.) Cook, stirring constantly, until mixture thickens slightly; strain. Allow custard to cool; stir in vanilla. Just before serving, spoon over peaches.

Serves 6

COOKIES

Unbaked Cookies

Combine in saucepan 2 cups sugar, 3 tablespoons cocoa, $^1/_2$ cup margarine and $^1/_2$ cup milk. Bring to boil and boil 2 minutes. Add $^1/_2$ cup peanut butter and 3 cups uncooked rolled oats. Stir well. Drop by teaspoonfuls on waxed paper; cool.

Makes about 4 dozen.

Refrigerator Nut Cookies

1 cup sugar
$^1/_2$ cup margarine
1 tsp. vanilla
1 egg, beaten

$1^3/_4$ cups sifted flour
2 tsp. baking powder
$^1/_4$ tsp. salt
$^1/_2$ cup chopped nuts

Cream butter and sugar, add vanilla and egg. Add sifted flour, baking powder and salt, mixing well. Stir in nuts. Form into long roll and wrap in wax paper. Chill overnight. Cut in thin slices and put on ungreased cookie sheet. Bake in 375°-oven for 10-12 minutes.

Makes about 40 cookies.

Chocolate Pinwheels

Prepare Refrigerator Nut Cookie recipe, above. Divide dough into two parts, adding 1 ounce melted chocolate to one part. Roll white and dark dough separately, $^1/_8$-inch thick. Place chocolate on top of vanilla dough, roll jell-roll fashion. Follow directions for Refrigerator Nut Cookies.

Easy Drop Cookies

2 eggs
$^3/_4$ cup shortening
$^1/_2$ cup brown sugar
1 tsp. soda

2 cups flour
1 cups white sugar
1 tsp. salt
1 tsp. vanilla

Slightly beat eggs. Cream in shortening, sugars, and remaining ingredients, adding the flour last. Drop from teaspoon onto ungreased sheet. Bake in 350°-oven until golden.

Oatmeal Cookies

1 cup sugar
1 cup shortening
1 cup raisins (boil in water for 10 minutes)
Pinch of salt
5 T. raisin liquid
1 tsp. soda
2 eggs

2 cups oatmeal
2 cups flour
1 tsp. cinnamon
$1/2$ tsp. nutmeg
1 tsp. vanilla
1 cup walnuts or pecans, chopped

Cream shortening and sugar; then add raisin liquid and eggs. Sift together the flour, soda, salt and spices and add to mixture. Stir in oatmeal, raisins, nuts, and vanilla. Drop from teaspoon onto baking sheets. Bake in moderate oven 350° for 8 to 10 minutes.

Picnic Cookie Sandwiches

$1/2$ cup shortening
$1/2$ cup sugar
1 egg
$2/3$ cup molasses
$2^{1}/2$ cups sifted flour
2 tsp. baking soda

1 tsp. ginger
$1/4$ tsp. cloves
$1/4$ tsp. allspice
$1/4$ tsp. salt
$1/2$ cup water

Cream together shortening and sugar; beat until light and fluffy. Beat in egg and molasses. Sift together flour, baking soda, ginger, cloves, allspice and salt. Add to creamed mixture alternately with water. Drop by heaping tablespoons onto greased baking sheet. Bake at 375° for 10 minutes. Cool on rack.

Spread half of the cookies with desired filling and cover with another cookie to form a sandwich. Store in a tightly covered container.

Makes 1 dozen sandwiches

Coconut Macaroons

3 egg whites
1 cup sugar
20 Ritz Crackers, crushed

½ cup pecans, chopped
½ cup coconut
1 tsp. vanilla

Beat egg whites until stiff, fold in sugar and cracker crumbs, pecans, coconut, and vanilla, one at a time. Bake at 350° until lightly browned. Cool before removing from baking sheet.

Toll House Oatmeal Cookies

¾ cup sifted flour
½ tsp. soda
½ tsp. salt
½ cup soft butter or shortening
6 T. granulated sugar
6 T. brown sugar
½ tsp. vanilla

¼ tsp. water
1 egg
1 cup oats, uncooked
1 (6-oz.) pkg. (1 cup) semi-
    sweet chocolate morsels

Heat oven to 375°. Sift together flour, soda and salt; set aside. Blend butter, sugars, vanilla and water. Beat in egg. Add flour mixture; mix well. Stir in oats and chocolate morsels. Drop by rounded half-teaspoons onto greased cookie sheets. Bake 10 to 12 minutes.

Fruit Cocktail Cookies

1 cup shortening
1 cup brown sugar
½ cup white sugar
1 tsp. soda
1 tsp. baking powder
4 cups flour

1 tsp. cinnamon
1 tsp. cloves
3 well beaten eggs
2 cups fruit cocktail (drained)
½ cup nuts
1 tsp. vanilla

Cream together shortening and sugars. Add eggs, fruit, nuts and vanilla. Sift together dry ingredients and add. Mix well. Drop from teaspoon onto baking sheet. Bake 8-10 minutes at 400°.

Texas Ranger Cookies

1 cup shortening
1 cup sugar
1 cup brown sugar
2 eggs
2 cups corn flakes
2 cups oatmeal

2 cups flour
2 tsp. soda
1 tsp. baking powder
$\frac{1}{2}$ tsp. salt
1 can coconut
1 tsp. vanilla

Cream shortening and sugars, add eggs. Stir in flakes and oats; add dry ingredients. Add vanilla and coconut. Drop from teaspoon onto cookie sheet. Bake 8 to 10 minutes at 375°.

Makes 6 dozen.

Old-Fashioned Tea Cakes

4 cups flour
4 tsp. baking powder
$\frac{1}{2}$ tsp. salt
1 cup shortening

2 tsp. vanilla
Milk
1 cup sugar
2 eggs

Sift dry ingredients together. Set aside. Cream shortening and sugar together till fluffy. Add eggs and continue beating. Add vanilla. Using just enough milk to form a stiff dough, add dry ingredients. Roll on floured board about $\frac{1}{4}$-inch thick. Do not grease cookie sheet. Cut in circles and bake at 350° until just brown around the edges.

Chocolate Drop Cakes

2 oz. bitter chocolate
$\frac{1}{2}$ cup shortening
1 egg, well beaten
1 cup light brown sugar
$\frac{1}{2}$ cup buttermilk
$1\frac{1}{2}$ cups sifted flour

$\frac{1}{4}$ tsp. baking powder
$\frac{1}{4}$ tsp. soda
$\frac{1}{4}$ tsp. salt
$\frac{1}{2}$ cup nuts, chopped
1 tsp. vanilla

Melt chocolate in double boiler over hot water. Add shortening and stir until creamy. Add egg, sugar, and buttermilk.

Sift dry ingredients together and add to first mixture. Add nuts and vanilla and drop mixture from teaspoon onto cookie sheet. Bake 350° for 10-12 minutes.

Applesauce Cookies

1 cup thick, unsweetened
   applesauce
1 cup sugar
1 egg
½ tsp. salt
1 tsp. soda
1 cup pecans, chopped
1 tsp. vanilla

1 tsp. baking powder
1 scant tsp. cloves
1 tsp. cinnamon
½ cup shortening
1 cup raisins
2 cups flour

Cream sugar and shortening until light and fluffy. Add applesauce and well beaten egg. Add raisins and pecans which have been dredged in ¼ cup of the measured flour. Add vanilla. Sift all dry ingredients together, add to mixture. Mix well and drop from teaspoon onto greased cookie sheet. Bake 15 minutes in 325°-oven.

CANDY

Great Peanut Butter Fudge

2 cups sugar
1 cup milk
Dash of salt

2 T. butter
1 tsp. vanilla
¾ cup chunky peanut butter

Boil sugar, milk and salt for 10 minutes; add butter. Continue boiling until mixture forms a soft ball in cold water. Remove from heat; add vanilla and peanut butter. Beat until mixture starts to set. Pour quickly into buttered pan. Cut into squares.

Pineapple Fudge

2 cups sugar
½ cup crushed pineapple, drained
½ cup thin cream

1 T. butter
½ cup chopped pecans

Mix all ingredients except pecans. Cook to soft-ball stage; cool. Beat until creamy, adding nuts. Pour into buttered square pan. Cool.

THE
WHOLE MEAL
FOR ABOUT
98¢

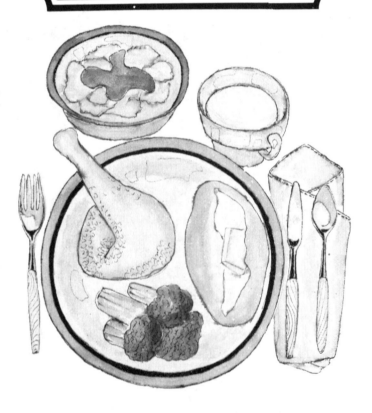

Serve each of these meals twice a month; average cost will not exceed 98¢ per serving. Each of these recipes serves 6.

Stuffed Beef Patties

1½ lbs. ground beef
¾ cup grated Cheddar cheese
3 T. chili sauce

3 T. drained pickle relish
Salt

Shape ground beef into 12 thin patties about 3½ inches in diameter. Combine cheese, chili sauce and pickle relish. Spoon cheese mixture on 6 of the patties, spreading to within ½ inch of edge. Top these with remaining patties and seal by pressing edges together. Broil 3 inches from heat for about 5 minutes on each side. Season with salt after cooking.

Approximate cost per serving 40¢.

Oven French-Fried Potatoes

6 medium potatoes cut in strips
1½ T. salad oil
Salt

Preheat oven to 450°. Coat potato strips with oil in a bowl. Place potato strips in a single layer in a large baking pan and bake for 35 minutes. Turn once after 25 minutes. Season with salt.

Cabbage and Carrot Salad

2½ cups finely shredded
    cabbage
1 cup grated raw carrots

1 medium green pepper,
    chopped
1 tsp. salt
¼ cup mayonnaise

Combine cabbage, carrots and green pepper in a bowl. Sprinkle with salt. Add mayonnaise and blend mixture together by tossing lightly.

Approximate cost per serving 10¢.

Blueberry Crumble

1 cup graham cracker crumbs
1/4 cup sugar
1/4 tsp. nutmeg
3 T. margarine, melted

2 cups frozen blueberries
1 tsp. lemon juice
1/2 tsp. vanilla
Vanilla ice cream

Combine graham cracker crumbs, sugar and nutmeg in a bowl. Add margarine and mix well. Place a layer of blueberries in a greased 1-quart shallow baking dish. Sprinkle with a layer of crumb mixture. Continue layering with berries and crumb mixture until ingredients are used ending with crumb layer. Drizzle with lemon juice and vanilla. Bake in a 350°-oven for 30 minutes. Serve topped with ice cream.

Approximate cost per serving 18¢.

TOTAL PER MEAL COST 78¢.

Hake Fillet

1 lb. fresh hake*
1 egg, slightly beaten
Cornmeal

Dip fillets in egg and roll in cornmeal. Pan fry until golden brown on both sides. Don't overcook. Serves 4-6.

Approximate cost per serving 38¢.

* Hake is a meaty, tasty, and inexpensive cod-fillet. If hake is not available in your area, other cod-type fillets may be substituted.

Parslied Potatoes and Carrots

4 medium potatoes
4 medium carrots
2 tsp. salt

4 T. margarine
2 T. chopped parsley

Heat about 2 cups of water plus 2 teaspoons salt to boiling in a saucepan. Wash, peel and cut potatoes and carrots into large pieces and add to water. Cover and heat to boiling. Reduce heat and simmer until vegetables are tender (about 20 minutes). Drain. Add margarine and parsley and toss gently.

Approximate cost per serving 10¢.

Tomato Aspic Salad

1½ T. gelatin	1 tsp. celery seed
3 cups tomato juice	1 tsp. minced, dried onion
½ tsp. salt	6 T. mayonnaise
¼ tsp. pepper	6 lettuce leaves

Soak gelatin in ½ cup tomato juice for about 5 minutes. Heat remainder of tomato juice with salt, pepper, celery seed, and minced dry onion to boiling. Add gelatin and tomato juice mixture, stir thoroughly until gelatin melts. Pour into six individual molds or a ring mold. Chill in refrigerator until firm. Serve on lettuce leaves. Garnish with mayonnaise.

Approximate cost per serving 13¢.

Apple Upside-Down Gingerbread

2 medium apples	½ cup brown sugar, firmly packed
2 T. margarine	1 (14-oz.) pkg. gingerbread mix

Wash, peel, core and slice apples. Melt margarine in an 8 x 8 x 2-inch baking pan. Stir in brown sugar until well mixed. Spread mixture evenly over bottom of pan. Arrange apple slices in sugar mixture. Prepare gingerbread according to package directions. Pour gingerbread batter over apples. Bake at 350° 35 to 40 minutes. Loosen gingerbread from sides of pan and invert onto serving plate. Serve warm.

Approximate cost per serving 18¢.

TOTAL PER MEAL COST 79¢.

Fruited Ham

½ cup regular rice
12 thin slices, boiled ham
¾ cup brown sugar
1 tsp. cornstarch
Juice of 1 orange
Juice of 1 lemon

½ cup water
Grated rind of 1 orange
⅛ tsp. cloves
½ cup whole cranberry sauce
¾ cup pineapple chunks

Cook rice according to package directions. Place cooked rice in greased 1½ quart casserole. Top with ham slices. Combine sugar and cornstarch in saucepan. Add orange and lemon juices, water, orange rind and cloves. Mix well, bring to boil, and simmer 3 minutes. Add cranberry sauce and pineapple. Simmer 5 minutes. Pour over ham and bake in 350°-oven until heated through, about 15 minutes.

Approximate cost per serving 40¢.

Spinach Salad

1 (10-oz.) pkg. fresh spinach
6 raw mushrooms, sliced
2 T. wine vinegar

6 T. oil
⅛ tsp. salt
⅛ tsp. pepper
1 T. salad herbs

Wash spinach and shake dry. Tear leaves into bite-sized pieces, discarding stems. Place spinach in a salad bowl. Wash mushrooms and slice them over spinach. Combine vinegar, oil, salt, pepper and herbs in a small jar. Cover and shake until thoroughly mixed. Pour dressing over salad just before serving.

Approximate cost per serving 26¢.

Minted Lemon Freeze

½ cup evaporated milk
1 egg, separated
4 T. lemon juice
½ cup sugar
½ tsp. lemon rind

½ tsp. peppermint extract
Pinch of salt
4 graham crackers, crushed
6 sprigs of fresh mint

Chill milk in a freezer tray until it begins to freeze. Place in mixer bowl and beat at high speed. Add egg white and 2 tablespoons lemon juice. Beat until stiff. Add sugar, egg yolk, remaining lemon juice, lemon rind, salt and peppermint extract. Beat on low speed until thoroughly blended. Place in freezer tray and sprinkle with graham cracker crumbs. Freeze until firm. Serve garnished with mint leaves.

Approximate cost per serving 13¢.

TOTAL PER MEAL COST 79¢.

Stuffed Acorn Squash

3 medium acorn squash
1½ lbs. ground beef
1 egg
½ cups soft bread crumbs

1 cup reconstituted instant
   nonfat dry milk
1 T. Worcestershire sauce
1 tsp. salt
2 tsp. dry mustard

Halve and remove seeds from squash. Parboil for 10 to 15 minutes. Combine the remaining ingredients and fill squash centers with mixture. Place in a greased baking pan. Bake at 350° for 45 minutes.

Approximate cost per serving 44¢.

Baked Potato Strips

6 medium potatoes
4 T. margarine, melted

⅔ cup crushed cornflakes

Pare and cut potatoes lengthwise into eighths. Dip in melted margarine and then in crushed cornflakes. Place on a greased cookie sheet. Bake in a 350°-oven 1 hour.

Approximate cost per serving 13¢.

Winter Fruit Compote

1 golden delicious apple
2 pears
1/2 cup seedless grapes
1 banana, sliced

1 orange, sectioned
1/2 grapefruit, sectioned
1 cup ginger ale

Quarter apple and pears; cut in bite-size pieces. Combine with grapes, banana slices, and orange and grapefruit sections in a small bowl. Toss gently. Cover and chill. Just before serving spoon into sherbet glasses and pour chilled ginger ale over fruits.

Approximate cost per serving 16¢.

TOTAL PER MEAL COST 73¢.

Cod Italiano

2 lbs. cod, fresh or frozen
1 onion, chopped fine
1 clove garlic, crushed

1 T. parsley, chopped
1/2 tsp. oregano
1 (16-oz.) can stewed tomatoes

Place fish in large skillet. Season with salt and pepper. Sprinkle with onion, garlic, parsley and oregano. Add tomatoes, crushing them with a fork. Cook over low heat, simmering gently until fish is tender and flakes, about 15-20 minutes.

Approximate cost per serving 51¢.

Peas and Corn

1 (10-oz.) pkg. frozen peas
1 (10-oz.) pkg. frozen corn

1 T. margarine
1/2 tsp. salt

Cook peas in salted water, according to package directions. Add corn and margarine. Continue cooking about 2-3 minutes.

Approximate cost per serving 11¢.

Linguini Rice

2 T. margarine
¼ cup linguini broken into
small pieces
1 cup uncooked regular rice

1 beef bouillon cube dissolved
in ½ cup hot water
1 tsp. salt
2½ cups water

Melt margarine in a 2-quart saucepan. Add linguini and brown lightly. Add remaining ingredients; bring to a boil. Cover pan. Reduce heat and let simmer for 25 minutes, or until all the liquid is absorbed.

Approximate cost per serving 6¢.

Orange and Banana Compote

4 oranges
2 bananas, sliced
½ cup orange marmalade

¾ cup sour cream
1 tsp. cinnamon

Peel and section oranges. Arrange orange sections with sliced bananas in individual serving dishes. Melt marmalade over hot water and spoon over fruit. Top with sour cream and sprinkle each serving dish with cinnamon.

Approximate cost per serving 19¢.

TOTAL PER MEAL COST 87¢.

Oven-Fried Fish Fillet

2 fish fillets, fresh or frozen
(approximately 1 lb. each)
2 tsp. salt

¾ cup seasoned bread crumbs
¼ cup Cheddar cheese, grated
¼ cup margarine, melted

Wash fish (frozen fillets do not have to be thawed), salt both sides. Sprinkle a greased flat casserole with half the bread crumbs. Place fish in casserole. Sprinkle cheese and remainder of bread crumbs over fish. Pour melted margarine over dish. Bake in 350°-oven about 15-20 minutes or until fish flakes when touched with a fork.

Approximate cost per serving 60¢.

Baked Potatoes

Wash 6 medium potatoes, prick skin with a fork to let steam escape during baking. Bake in 350°-oven for about 1½ or until potatoes are soft when pressed. Cut criss-cross gash across potato tops and insert 1 tablespoon butter or margarine. Garnish with a sprig of parsley.

Approximate cost per serving 8¢.

Grilled Tomatoes

3 medium tomatoes
Salt and pepper
½ clove garlic, minced
2 T. bread crumbs
1 T. butter or margarine

Cut tomatoes in halves and place on baking pan. Sprinkle with salt, pepper, and bread crumbs. Dot with butter or margarine. Broil until bread crumbs are brown.

Approximate cost per serving 10¢.

Ambrosia

2 medium oranges, sectioned
(or ¾ cup Mandarin orange slices)
¾ cup pineapple chunks

2 large bananas, sliced
¾ cup flaked coconut

Combine oranges, pineapple, bananas, and coconut in a serving dish. Chill thoroughly in refrigerator. Serve cold.

Approximate cost per serving 9¢.

TOTAL PER MEAL COST 87¢.

Swiss Steak

1½ lb. boneless, chuck-
    shoulder steak
¼ cup flour
1 tsp. salt
½ tsp. pepper

2 T. oil
1 (28-oz.) can tomatoes
1 small onion, chopped
½ cup water

Place steak on a wooden board. Slash fat edges to prevent curling. Sift flour, salt, and pepper together. Pound flour mixture thoroughly into steak on both sides with a wooden mallet. Heat oil in a heavy skillet, add steak and brown on both sides. Add tomatoes with juice, onion and water. Cover tightly and simmer on top of stove or bake in a 325°-oven for 2 hours.

Approximate cost per serving 56¢.

Baked Noodles

1 (12-oz.) pkg. noodles
1 tsp. salt

2 T. margarine
4 cups boiling water

Place noodles in an ungreased 2-quart casserole. Sprinkle with salt. Add margarine. Pour boiling water over noodles and mix thoroughly. Cover and bake in 325°-oven until tender, about 35 to 40 minutes.

Approximate cost per serving 10¢.

Three-Bean Salad

1 (15½-oz.) can green beans
1 (15½-oz.) can wax beans
1 (16-oz.) can kidney beans
1 medium onion, chopped

½ cup sugar
⅔ cup vinegar
⅓ cup oil
1 tsp. salt
1 tsp. pepper

Drain beans and place in bowl. Add chopped onion. Combine sugar, vinegar, salad oil, salt and pepper. Pour mixture over beans, cover, and refrigerate for at least 12 hours. Serve on lettuce or other salad greens. (This mixture keeps well in the refrigerator for several days.)

Approximate cost per serving 16¢.

Cranberry Baked Apples

6 large baking apples
3/4 cup chopped, raw
   cranberries

1/2 cup sugar
3 T. chopped walnuts
1/2 cup water

Wash and core apples. Slit the skin around apples about halfway down. Combine chopped cranberries, sugar and chopped nuts. Stuff apples with cranberry mixture. Place apples in baking dish. Pour water around apples to prevent sticking. Bake in 325°-oven until tender (1 to 1 1/2 hours). Serve warm or chilled.

Approximate cost per serving 17¢.

TOTAL PER MEAL COST 99¢.

Creamed Chicken and Peas

3 T. margarine
2 T. green pepper, chopped
5 T. flour
1 chicken bouillon cube
1 1/2 cups water

1 1/4 cup reconstituted instant
   nonfat dry milk
3 cups diced cooked chicken
1 cup cooked frozen peas
1 tsp. salt
1/2 tsp. mace

Melt margarine in a 2-quart saucepan. Add green pepper and cook until tender. Blend in the flour. Add bouillon cube, water and milk. Cook to a smooth mixture, stirring constantly. Mix in chicken, peas, salt, and mace. Heat thoroughly.

Approximate cost per serving 57¢.

Gourmet Rice

1 cup regular rice, uncooked
2 1/2 cups water
1 beef bouillon cube

1 tsp. salt
2 T. margarine
1/2 cup grated process cheese

Boil 3 cups water in a 2-quart saucepan. Add bouillon cube, rice, salt and margarine. Cover and cook until liquid is absorbed. Before serving, sprinkle with grated cheese.

Approximate cost per serving 10¢.

Lemony Broccoli

2 (10-oz.) pkg. frozen broccoli   2 T. margarine
    spears   Juice of 1 medium lemon
1 tsp. salt

Cook broccoli in salted water, according to directions. Melt margarine and add lemon juice. Pour over broccoli and serve.

Approximate cost per serving 16¢.

Fresh Fruit Compote

¼ cup butter or margarine   ½ cup orange juice
½ cup confectioner's sugar   ¾ cup each, orange sections,
1 T. cornstarch   sliced pears, sliced apples,
2 T. lemon juice   sliced bananas
2 tsp. orange rind, grated   6 T. vanilla ice cream

Combine margarine, sugar, cornstarch, lemon juice, orange rind, and orange juice in a chafing dish or 2-quart saucepan. Cook, stirring constantly, until slightly thick. Stir in fruit. Simmer just until fruit is warm. Serve immediately in sherbert glasses and garnish each serving with 1 tablespoon vanilla ice cream.

Approximate cost per serving 23¢.

TOTAL PER MEAL COST $1.06

Grilled Fish in Foil

2 lbs. frozen fish fillets   ½ tsp. pepper
3 medium onions, sliced thin   Pinch of thyme, tarragon and
3 medium tomatoes, chopped   dried parsley
1 tsp. salt   4 T. margarine

Thaw fish fillets in refrigerator. Place fish on heavy duty foil. Top with onion slices. Add tomatoes, salt, pepper, herbs and margarine. Wrap foil tightly, making sure edges are secure. Grill over low fire (gray-hot coals) for 30 to 35 minutes, turning once half way through cooking.

Approximate cost per serving 60¢.

Pasta Salad

6 oz. elbow macaroni
2 cups frozen carrots and peas
2 T. dehydrated onion flakes
2 T. dill seed
2 tsp. salt

¼ tsp. pepper
¾ cup mayonnaise
¾ cup milk
6 lettuce leaves

Cook macaroni according to package directions. Drain. Cook carrots and peas in a small amount of water. Drain. Cool macaroni and vegetables in refrigerator. After cooling combine macaroni, vegetables, onion flakes, dill seed, salt and pepper in a large bowl. Add mayonnaise and milk. Mix well. Refrigerate several hours. Serve on lettuce leaves.

Approximate cost per serving 23¢.

Eggplant Slices

1 medium eggplant
2 T. olive oil
2 T. grated Cheddar cheese

1 tsp. salt
½ tsp. pepper
1 tsp. thyme

Wash eggplant and dry. Cut it into 6 slices and brush with olive* oil. Place slices on heavy-duty foil and broil for about 8 minutes. Turn and sprinkle with cheese, salt and pepper. Broil for about 5 minutes longer. Before serving, sprinkle with thyme.

*Be sure to use *olive* oil. It provides an unmistakable mellowness.

Approximate cost per serving 10¢.

Strawberry Cream Pie

¾ cup reconstituted frozen
    orange juice, cold
1 envelope unflavored gelatin

¼ tsp. grated orange peel
1 pint strawberry ice cream
1 eight-inch baked pie shell

Pour cold orange juice into a 1-quart sauce pan. Sprinkle gelatin over juice to soften it. Stir mixture over moderate heat until gelatin dissolves. Remove from heat. Add ice cream and orange peel to hot mixture and stir until melted and smooth. Pour into baked pie shell and chill until firm.

Approximate cost per serving 18¢.

TOTAL PER MEAL COST $1.11

Braised Lamb Shoulder Chops

6 (½-inch thick) lamb shoulder chops
1½ tsp. salt
½ tsp. pepper

Pinch of garlic salt
1½ T. lemon juice
3 T. water

Brown chops on both sides in a skillet. Combine remaining ingredients and pour over chops. Cover and simmer 30 minutes, turning once after 15 minutes.

Approximate cost per serving 73¢.

Mashed Potatoes with Chives

6 medium potatoes
½ cup reconstituted instant nonfat dry milk

3 T. butter or margarine
3 T. dehydrated chives
Salt and pepper

Wash and peel potatoes. Cover with boiling water and cook with salt in covered saucepan until tender. Drain, add butter or margarine, salt and pepper. Mash. Add milk and chives. Whip until fluffy.

Approximate cost per serving 10¢.

French Green Beans

2 pkgs. frozen French-style
   green beans
1 beef bouillon cube

½ tsp. pepper
1 tsp. salt
½ tsp. dried basil

Cook beans according to directions, adding bouillon cube to water. Drain. Season with salt, pepper, and basil.

Approximate cost per serving 13¢.

Quick Banana Pudding

1 pkg. vanilla pudding mix
3 medium bananas sliced

24 vanilla wafers, broken or
   crushed
½ cup toasted coconut

Prepare pudding according to directions on the package. Place alternate layers of bananas, wafers, and pudding in parfait glasses or serving dishes. Top with toasted coconut.

Approximate cost per serving 16¢.

TOTAL PER MEAL COST $1.12

Turkey and Potato Casserole

3 T. margarine
3 T. flour
½ tsp. salt
¼ tsp. pepper
¼ tsp. paprika
2 cups reconstituted nonfat dry
   milk

2 T. chopped green onions
3 cups diced, cooked potatoes
3 cups diced, cooked turkey
½ cup bread crumbs
2 T. chopped parsley

Melt margarine in a 1-quart saucepan. Blend in flour, salt, pepper and paprika. Gradually add milk and cook, stirring constantly, until mixture thickens and comes to a boil. Remove from heat. Stir in green onions. Pour sauce into a 1½-quart casserole. Add potatoes and turkey. Mix well. Top with bread crumbs. Bake in a 350°-oven for 30 minutes or until heated through. Garnish with chopped parsley.

Approximate cost per serving 69¢.

Peas and Mushrooms

2 (10-oz.) pkgs. frozen peas
½ tsp. salt
1 small onion, diced

1 T. margarine
1 (4-oz.) can mushroom stems and pieces

Cook peas in salted water according to package directions. Drain. Meanwhile, saute onions in margarine until lightly browned. Combine peas and mushrooms with onions.

Approximate cost per serving 18¢.

Tossed Salad

1 small head, lettuce
½ lb. fresh spinach

1 medium carrot, grated
½ cup Italian dressing

Wash salad greens. Drain. Dry on a cloth or paper towel. Tear leaves into pieces that can be handled easily with a fork. Place greens in a large bowl, add grated carrots. Refrigerate. Just before serving add Italian dressing and toss lightly.

Approximate cost per serving 17¢.

Low-Calorie Orange Whip

1 T. plain gelatin
¼ cup sugar
½ cup water
1 (6-oz.) can frozen orange juice

½ cup ice water
⅔ cup instant nonfat dry milk
2 T. sugar
1 T. lemon juice

Mix gelatin, sugar and ½ cup water in a saucepan. Stir over low heat until dissolved. Remove from heat. Stir in undiluted frozen orange juice. Chill until mixture is the consistency of an unbeaten egg white. Put ice water in a small bowl. Stir in dry milk. Beat until peak forms. Beat in lemon juice and remaining sugar. Fold into the gelatin mixture. Chill.

Approximate cost per serving 11¢.

TOTAL PER MEAL COST $1.15

Savory Pork Chops

6 pork chops
¾ tsp. salt
¼ tsp. pepper
6 thin slices lemon

6 tsp. brown sugar
½ tsp. oregano
½ cup catsup

Place chops in baking dish. Sprinkle with salt and pepper. Top each chop with a slice of lemon and sprinkle with brown sugar and oregano. Pour catsup over chops. Bake for about 1 hour in a 325°-oven.

Approximate cost per serving 82¢.

Speedy Cheesey Potatoes

6 servings, instant mashed
   potatoes
¾ T. dried onion flakes
1 tsp. salt

⅛ tsp. pepper
½ cup grated mild Cheddar
   cheese

Prepare potatoes according to package directions adding onion flakes, salt, and pepper. Spread potatoes in greased baking dish. Sprinkle with cheese. Bake in a 325°-oven for 10 minutes or until cheese melts.

Approximate cost per serving 10¢.

Parslied Carrots

8 medium carrots
1 T. margarine

2 T. water
¼ cup chopped parsley

Wash, peel and cut carrots in strips. Place carrots in a greased baking dish, dot with margarine, add water. Cover and bake 1 hour in a 325°-oven. Garnish with chopped parsley.

Approximate cost per serving 8¢.

Cherry Cobbler

1 (21-oz.) can cherry pie filling
½ tsp. vanilla
2 cups biscuit mix

½ cup reconstituted nonfat dry
   milk
1 T. sugar

Mix pie filling and vanilla in a square pan, 8 x 8 x 2 inches. Combine biscuit mix, milk, and sugar in a bowl. Stir until dough forms a ball and cleans the bowl. Drop dough by spoonfuls over cherries. Bake in a 325°-oven 35 to 40 minutes or until golden brown. Serve warm.

Approximate cost per serving 20¢.

TOTAL PER MEAL COST $1.20

Beef Brisket Rosemary

3-3½ lbs. fresh beef brisket	1 tsp. salt
1 clove garlic, crushed	½ tsp. pepper
1 cup tomato juice	¼ tsp. rosemary

Place meat in shallow glass or glazed pan. Combine other ingredients, mix well and pour over meat. Pierce meat deeply with a sharp fork on all sides. Cover and marinate in refrigerator 2 to 3 hours; turn meat several times. Drain. Place meat in roasting pan, cover with foil and roast in 325°-oven for 2½ hours. Let cool before slicing.

Approximate cost per serving 90¢.

Scalloped Potatoes

6 medium potatoes	2 T. butter or margarine
2 large onions	2 cups reconstituted instant
Salt and pepper	nonfat dry milk
2 T. flour	

Wash, peel and cut potatoes into thin slices. Peel and thinly slice onions. Alternate layers of potatoes and onions in a large greased baking dish. Sprinkle each layer with salt, pepper and flour. Pour in milk until it comes just to top layer; dot with butter or margarine. Cover and bake in a 325°-oven for 1 hour. Uncover and bake ½ hour longer or until tender and browned.

Approximate cost per serving 9¢.

Harvard Beets

2 (16-oz.) cans sliced beets
½ cup cider vinegar

1 T. cornstarch
4 T. sugar

Blend cornstarch and sugar in saucepan. Add vinegar and cook over medium heat until it begins to thicken, stirring constantly. Add beets and continue stirring to prevent sticking until heated thoroughly.

Approximate cost per serving 14¢.

Apple Crisp

4 cups pared and sliced tart
  apples
2 T. sugar
¼ tsp. cinnamon
¼ cup water

½ cup flour
⅛ tsp. salt
¼ tsp. nutmeg
⅓ cup brown sugar
3 T. margarine

Mix sugar, cinnamon, and apples in a mixing bowl. Spread apples in a greased 8 x 8-inch baking pan and sprinkle with water.

Blend remaining ingredients together and spread over apples. Bake uncovered in a 325°-oven for 1 hour or until lightly browned and apples are tender.

Approximate cost per serving 11¢.

TOTAL PER MEAL COST $1.24

INDEX

MEAT, POULTRY, FISH

ONE-DISH WONDERS

WHOLE MEAL FOR ABOUT 98¢, THE (per person)